BROCKHAMPTON PRESS
LONDON

© 1996 Geddes & Grosset Ltd, David Dale House,
New Lanark ML11 9DJ

This edition published 1996 by Brockhampton Press,
a member of the Hodder Headline PLC Group

ISBN 1 86019 326 9

Printed and bound in India

Contents

Introduction   9
Clairvoyance and Crystal-gazing   11
Tea-leaf Fortunes   21
Dice and Good Luck   27
Fortune-telling by Dominoes   30
Fortune-telling by Numbers   33
Weather Fortunes   39
The Months and their Fortune   43
Fortune-telling by the Cards   51
Palmistry   98
Superstitions   144

Introduction

There are many secrets to be revealed through the ancient arts of fortune-telling. One of the most popular and perhaps most immediately recognizable is that of crystal gazing—a form of divination that has been practised from earliest times.

The first chapter of this book looks at clairvoyance and crystal gazing, tracing its history through to modern times, and gives a background to the practice and its interpretations.

In the same way, telling the future by reading tea leaves introduces a favourite, lighter form of divination. Predicting the future by reading tea leaves may have decreased with the use of the tea bag, but it still has a following, and there is an explanation here of the procedure to be followed for reading the leaves, with discussion of the symbols and their meanings.

Dice and dominoes have been used for many games of chance and fortune thoughout history. Instructions are clearly laid down with common interpretations to allow this form of divination to be tested. There is an introduction to fortune-telling by numbers, weather and the months, which complete the first part of this book.

Card-reading is another popular way of fortune-telling, and the second part of the book provides an introduction to the suits and the individual cards, revealing their meanings both singly and in combination.

The third part of the book looks at the ancient art of palmistry, foretelling what will happen by interpreting the lines and marks on the human hand.

Finally, there is a section on superstitions, belief in which can give us the idea that we can, to some degree at least, see what lies ahead.

Clairvoyance and Crystal-gazing

'Clairvoyance', originally a French word, means 'the ability to see clearly'. The reason so few people possess this extraordinary psychic faculty is because many human beings are insensitive to anything beyond the ordinary emotions. The power of prophecy and acute intuition is a sixth sense, which most of us have to a slight degree but which often remains dormant and uncultivated.

Clairvoyance has often been mistaken for superstition or wilfully imposed and cunning deceptions, but it has stood firm through the ages in spite of the quackery of wizards, the paraphernalia of sorcerers (used to inspire fear and awe in the uninitiated) or the sneers of the materialistic. All of us at some time or other have felt the control of that still small voice, as potent and penetrating as conscience, which comes to instil us with awe, joy, sadness or warning at some critical juncture of our lives, often anticipating, with a power greater than speech can convey, some event that concerns our wellbeing.

Science teaches that a million delicate sounds escape the ear and brain, and as many minute exquisitely fashioned atoms escape the eye. A magnifying glass reveals the structure of insects and microbes invisible to the naked eye, and it is only by means of a telescope that the beauty of the stars is discerned. In this way the developed power of clairvoyance can be called the magnifying lens of the soul. It is perhaps because this lens is dull and misty that we fail to see.

History and literature go a long way towards proving its existence. Many of the stories and prophecies of the Bible are founded on clairvoyance. People were simpler and more trusting then, and for this reason it is said that visions and clear sight were granted to them.

Pilate's disregard of the warning conveyed in his wife's dream affected the course of Christianity, and the Bible abounds with examples of the disasters that befell those who disobeyed the spiritual promptings sent to them.

Colour and Character

Clairvoyance teaches that everybody has a distinctive colour, an aura, which conveys more of character and personality than any word or action. The shades of these colours vary according to temperament and are as much concealed from the untrained eye as the million tints composing the gold, purple and green bands of the rainbow.

Optimistic people give out a pale blue aura.
Large-minded, progressive people, a pale green.
Pessimistic, worried people, grey.
Ill-health in mind or body, dark green.
Kindly, benevolent, humane people, pink.
The thinker and scholar, deep blue.
The degraded, brown.
The passionate and bad-tempered, red.
The ambitious, orange.
The lover of beauty in art, yellow.

These colours, however, although providing the key to the character are subject to constant changes. Our moods sway and change our thoughts according to the happenings that affect us.

For example, bereavement or anxiety has the power to transform the blue aura of the optimistic temperament to grey, and this temporary change of colour studied alone may puzzle the clairvoyant and lead to a false diagnosis of character.

To prevent this, the seer should request that some article constantly worn by the enquirer be made available, the older and shabbier the better. A glove, an everyday tie, a ring that is constantly worn are equally valuable as a means to discriminate between the temporary aura and the habitual aura specific to the temperament.

For example, when a man's glove emits a pale blue aura, in contradiction to the grey of his own personality, the deduction is that he is naturally of a hopeful and cheerful tendency but that some mental anxiety or grief causes the grey, deep or pale, according to the depth of the emotion dominating him.

The reason for this difference of colours is that the glove is, as it were, saturated with the essence of his normal disposition, while the colour of his character has been changed by circumstances or environment.

People of erratic temperament possess an aura of many and constantly changing colours, but those who have a calm temperament that rarely varies maintain only one.

A few people are aware of the tones of their aura and are therefore sensitive to the influence of their surroundings. They will be quite miserable if the paper on their walls, or the materials of their clothes, clashes in colour with that of their character, while they are at their best and happiest surrounded by the tints that blend or contrast harmoniously.

The clairvoyant possesses six key qualities:

1. The power of magnetism.
2. Mental health and influence.
3. Physical health and cleanliness.
4. Moderation in food and drink.
5. The power of discerning the aura and interpreting its colours.
6. Freedom from bad habits.

In advanced clairvoyance the use of the crystal for seeing is designated by many seers as 'claptrap' and thought to be a vulgar 'playing to the gallery'. It is known to be bad for the eyes to gaze at any shining article for too long a time, yet in clairvoyance there is no doubt that it aids the concentration of sight and thought.

By means of crystal-gazing, the seer creates and becomes subject to the influence of autohypnosis—the ability to become entranced, which veils his or her own personality, forming a link to the client.

The surface of the crystal gradually reflects images and subconscious impressions conveyed by and vital to the individual whose past, present and future are being revealed.

Sympathy and intuition merge the gazer's aura with the temperamental colouring of the client. The seer's magnetic force creates further powers, while the sixth sense is the nucleus about which these are bound.

No student of clairvoyance can be successful in discerning character and personal emanations of colour unless disciplined by simple rules that should govern his or her life.

Excessive eating, drinking, over-indulgence in any form, self-indulgence, bad habits and drugs destroy this delicate sixth sense. Lack of sincerity and integrity result in the rapid decline of its power. The body and mind must be pure and of perfect mental and physical balance.

When consulting a clairvoyant, the client should be serious and earnest, and trust that the truth will be heard. Frivolity, incredulity or idle curiosity forms a thick crust between the minds of the seer and the enquirer that prevents the penetrating of thoughts and vision, strains the powers, and results in disappointment.

The clairvoyant should be approached in the same way in which one visits a doctor or solicitor, and there must be no determined reserve to conceal thoughts and character in the mind.

Clairvoyance in a room full of people is extremely difficult—indeed impossible unless the onlookers can keep perfectly quiet.

It is always better to be alone with the enquirer in a small room where traffic noises do not penetrate, provided only with the necessary furniture, kept clean and fresh, airy and well lighted.

The crystal should never be touched by anyone except the clairvoyant and must be kept free from spots and smudges. A black silk handkerchief around its globe will be a help to fortune-telling by preventing the reflection of lights.

There may be, especially for beginners, a temptation to pose as the possessor of supernatural powers—to gesticulate over the crystal, light wax tapers, burn perfumes and murmur incantations—but these methods, although employed by the ancient prophets, are of no help to the modern seer. Indeed, they do harm by appealing to the senses and superstitions, and, being mere affectation, are unworthy of that sixth sense and harmful to it.

The simpler the manifestation, the more assured the clairvoyant may be of arriving at the truth.

Self-confidence, an absolute belief in the gift and faith in method must rule.

The seer does not try to avoid nervous exertion by discreetly 'pumping' the enquirer as to ways and means but takes delight in silent investigation.

The clairvoyant should come to the task fresh and buoyant, bubbling with enthusiasm. At the slightest sense of tiredness the seer should halt all efforts, as it is extremely harmful to apply any force or strain to this abstract power.

Physical fatigue and excitement must be avoided, for these lead to jangled nerves, sleeplessness, and finally an inability to isolate the mind from the orbit of our own concerns to the sphere of others.

The processes that occur in crystal-gazing are thought transference and telepathy. A communication of ideas is set up between the clairvoyant and client, and the mirror-like surface of the crystal is the medium by which innate thoughts are reflected.

As far as possible, the clairvoyant submerges his or her own personality in that of the enquirer. Profound silence brings about the sense of atmosphere and aura, and this, coupled with intent gazing into the crystal, brings about the visions that the clairvoyant interprets.

The crystal is supposed to be the magic bridge that gulfs the chasm fixed between itself and the spiritual world. In the iron it contains are situated the collective and culminating forces.

Mists of white, green, blue and violet tints are symbols of good fortune and happiness. Black, yellow and red are warnings of disaster. When the mists disperse and gradually come to the surface, the clairvoyant may reply to any question in the affirmative. Mists that descend to the bottom are negative signs.

Images that develop to the left of the clairvoyant are real. Those on the right are purely symbolical.

In order to apply oneself to the achievement of reading the secret depths of mind, character, talent and circumstances, it is necessary to possess the ability to become separate from material surroundings and allow the spirit to dominate the body.

This can be achieved only by hypnotizing oneself. Clairvoyance is based on certain forms of this semi-somnolent state, for, just as in hypnotism, the mind reigns supreme over matter and becomes isolated by means of an object, so, in clairvoyance, a waking trance is brought about by a fixed gazing into the crystal.

However, there are other methods of inducing this state, some more and some less difficult until constant practice and experience make them a habit.

For the reason that gazing for a long time at a bright surface is harmful to eyesight, many clairvoyants prefer to create visions without the use of a crystal.

Words repeated over and over again have a mysterious power of isolating the sixth sense from the rest. For example, the word *aum* is extraordinarily symbolical. It stands for three influences: A = the Objective, U = the Subjective, M = the Eternal.

These are the kingdoms in the heart of the human being. The Objective represents the natural surroundings of objects and events that we all can feel and see. The Subjective is the realm of influences, the degree of which is felt according to the perception and training of our individual spiritual forces. Too often it is vague and elusive because most of us ignore its existence. The Eternal World is that state to which the subjective world in its highest state of development leads.

The word *aum* repeated, slowly and steadily at first and then at great speed, is said to have the ability to create, as it were, a vacuum between the spirit and body of the prophet. The mind dwells on its meaning, the vibration of the different letters acts on the mind, and the gazer is carried by gentle stages to the seat of his or her spiritual being.

It is when the seer attains this full development that large, clear and deep perceptions of the client's character are granted, and it is possible for him or her to reveal facts concerning the client that would be impossible in a normal state.

The sensation experienced is that of being plunged into space, in which the senses of sight, hearing and touch are transmuted to the brain and spirit.

The student will most probably be discouraged at first by an inability to produce this state, but it should be remembered that hard work and perseverance are the attributes that all must give to attain perfection in any learning, art or science. A person destined to become a great mathematician often stumbles with despair in childhood over the first addition sum, and the most distinguished musician has to do battle with the rudiments of music.

So it is in clairvoyance. Seemingly insuperable difficulties surround the novice who has never learnt to recognize the value and power of the sixth sense. Patience, a tranquil, determined mind, and not a little courage, are necessary. Time and growth work wonders in the persistent mind, and it will be seen that the obstacles gradually move aside, the curtain is lifted, and the seeker reaches that mature vision which he or she has formerly imagined dimly, if at all.

It is a good plan for the novice to ponder on his or her own name, and, shut away from all distractions, repeat it again and again aloud. The seer will gradually feel a sense of deep mystery, for in that name is concentrated the riddle of existence. The blending of spiritual and material kingdoms lies behind it, and the material slips rapidly into obscurity.

Only when the heart is pure and worthy will the vision

be granted—the clouds of bitterness, envy, hatred and malice that generally hide the precious jewel from the light and render brilliance impossible are discarded.

Everyone knows how difficult it is to control the mind and keep it from mean and uncharitable thoughts. It is more rebellious even than the body and influences it for good or evil.

Above all else, the clairvoyant must learn to discipline and constrain his or her thoughts. A humble outlook and a longing for purity and singleness of purpose are needed to bring about the most noble qualities, and it is here that proper treatment of the body is invaluable.

A simple diet, early rising, daily exercise, constant isolation and cultivation of good habits create the orbit for the higher faculties. These are the elementary rudiments of clairvoyance, and, unless they are mastered, the clairvoyant, no matter how diligent and persevering he or she may be in study and labour, will not succeed.

Tea-leaf Fortunes

The secret of success in this art consists of concentration, which enables the seer, who has a mind empty of all outside matters, to seize at a glance the symbols thrown up in the teacups and to read them intelligently so that the subject, or person whose cup is being read, can understand.

The cup must be passed directly to the seer by the person who has drunk the tea. If the cup passes from hand to hand before it reaches the seer, the fortune will be confused and undefined, and most likely untrue.

It is also desirable that the subject should sit near the seer when the cup has been given up. But the cup ought to be turned over on to the saucer to allow for 'tears' to be drained off the leaves before it is handed to the seer. It is extraordinary how tears, or drops of tea, will stay in the cup, however long it has remained turned over on the saucer, if there is matter for grief in the fortune of the subject.

Some subjects turn the cup round three times and touch the edge of the saucer with the cup, 'wishing the wish of the heart' as they do so. But unless there is a clear or outstanding star near the top on the inner side of the teacup, no more is heard of this 'wish of the heart'. (Wishes properly belong to card-reading.)

The seer or reader picks up the turned-over cup from the saucer, which the subject hands over.

You (if 'you' are the seer) hold the cup in your right hand. Note that the handle of the teacup is the house or home of the subject or 'place'. For someone whose interest is entirely in business, the handle may stand for 'the office'; for an actress it may mean 'the theatre', for a doctor, 'the surgery'. But for the average man or woman you will do well to read it as 'the home'.

The near or inner side of the cup, as you hold it in your right hand, is 'the fortune', the things that are happening or are sure to happen.

On the outer or farther side we read thoughts, things that may come, that are likely or possible but that are now very much 'in the air', unfulfilled, uncertain. If you read the same person's cup tomorrow or in a week's time, there may be quite a different story to be read from the outer side of the cup.

Some seers read a month's time in the depths of the cup, dividing it into two and reading the immediate fortnight that is coming from the top half, and the third and fourth weeks from now in the lower half of the cup's side. Happenings of a month ahead are near the bottom of the side. The very top is today. The rim is now. Close to the rim is by first post tomorrow morning. A leaf or sprig sticking out on the rim, startling news, now. Any sign sticking out implies surprise, even shock.

Note that the leaves or sprigs of tea dust—any combination of symbols, in fact—that lie on the bottom of the cup stand for trouble, annoyance, anxiety, mishap, bad luck, misfortune. Even if it is a star, it is a wish or a 'glory' that will cause the subject more sorrow than joy.

And drops, moisture, liquid, things that stand for 'tears' always cling to the bottom of the cup. Notice especially that whatever you read in the bottom of the cup is timed as *now*. This is all to the good. Your subject's cup may be quite clear at the bottom tomorrow!

Sometimes, especially if the seer is reading a person's cup for the first time, and more especially if they are meeting for the first time, the skilled reader will rule out all 'time' and will read from the cup a fortune that goes far ahead and may cover the whole life of the subject.

The most experienced reader of teacups cannot tell what it is that impels him or her to do this, but does know that he or she is actually and truly reading what is sure to come true, and feels, with the feeling that is stronger than all knowledge, that what is 'seen' must be said. This rare and inexplicable state of mind looks beyond all symbolism. Symbols are no longer there; for the seer is now really clairvoyant, seeing nothing, but 'telling' of what is surely in the veiled future.

The Meaning of the Symbols
All the signs explained here are to be read as important or negligible according to size and clearness. Signs that disappear almost as they are read are true things that are ceasing to matter.

animals horses and dogs are friends. A lion represents a powerful friend. A tiger is an unreliable rich man, not necessarily an enemy. Leopards and wolves are enemies. A cat or a cow is a deceitful woman. Monkeys are mischievous people, especially if they are grinning.

baby a sign that one may be expected. If a cradle is near it, all will be well.

birds if they are in flight, birds say that news is coming. A bird standing is not such a good sign. A bird standing on one leg indicates plans frustrated or things changed for the worse since news was received.

circles *see* RINGS.

crosses symbolize things earned. A large, well-made cross tells of painful ambition realized. A small or ill-made cross implies obstacles, with danger of losses. A cross beside a grave, a funeral. Near to a wreath of flowers, a death. Not 'near' if there are no tears in the bottom of the cup.

dots are news, but of things of the mind, scholarship, science. Dots set as a triangle denote a wish, a successful but not exactly a material one. Dots are 'fine' things, sometimes ideas. Dots set inside small circles are money through business or affairs.

faces these are described to the subject, saying whether they stand for men or women, old or young, sad or joyful people. The subject must identify them. Sometimes the subject's own face is formed clearly by dots. Notice its position and the signs near it. But the fact that it is there, means that the day or the time is important.

gardens represent flirtations.

hearts two hearts tell of an engagement. If there is a ring around them or near them, this denotes a happy marriage. A crown over the joined hearts is a very auspicious sign.

letters denote the arrival of something by post. A dot in

the middle of a square or 'long square' letter, tells of
money by post.

letters of the alphabet alphabet letters are often thrown
up in the teacup with astonishing clarity. These do not
always stand for the initials of a name; they may indicate a town. But two or three capital letters together are,
as a rule, the initials of someone with whom the subject
ought to get into communication. Figures must be read
in conjunction with the symbols that are near to it.

lines lines stand for distance. Two lines are journeys by
train or car. A ship is a voyage. Cars, engines and such
things stand for themselves, but notice how they are
placed and where.

masses or **heaps** masses or heaps of tea leaves are prosperity. The larger or higher they are, the more money or
good luck is indicated. But masses in the bottom of the
cup indicate that there is much anxiety even concerning
what should be unmitigated good.

rings if they are small, rings mean business offers; if
large, a proposal of marriage. Rings are always something that involves a question or an offer. A circle with a
letter near it says the offer will be made in writing.

A ring formed of dots denotes an offer that is not so
definite. A half or a part circle, not fully closed, is an in-
definite offer or a half-question thrown out as a 'feeler'
or with some hesitation. The same rule applying to
smallness or largeness applies to the complete ring. It
denotes business if small and marriage if large.

sprigs stand for people. Tightly curled sprigs are men,
and more loosely furled ones are women. When up-

standing, these are straightforward people, although if there is any kind of a weapon pointed at them, or from them, the message is 'Beware'. Sprigs set across are people who have been vexed. Look at the nearby symbols to find out why. Sprigs set sideways are people who are not quite trustworthy. People are also represented by faces, initials and signs, which the subject must identify.

squares tell of safety from a feared danger or deliverance. With a half-moon, squares denote danger of drowning escaped. But squares say that the subject is, for the time being, 'taking one step forward and two steps backwards' and, at best, is merely 'marking time', even if the square is set in the clear of the cup's side.

stars indicate successes, desires fulfilled, 'glory' achieved and startling success. If they appear in the bottom, something in the nature of fatality accompanies the good happenings.

triangles symbolize prevention of ill or trouble avoided. Look at the symbols nearby to interpret these more fully.

Enough has been said to show how the teacups ought to be read. 'The way to do it, is to do it.' A last word to the would-be seer: Never hesitate to say what you see clearly in the cup you are reading.

If you are sincere (selfless) in the matter and the subject is intelligent and anxious to know things, what you say is sure to be true or to come true.

Dice and Good Luck

Dice have been used for many games of chance and fortune throughout history. From ancient Egypt and classical Greece to the Far East, numbered cubes made of wood, glass, ivory or metal with their sides inscribed from 1–6 were popular for games and as a means of consultation. It was found through their medium that future happenings and events could be predicted.

Test this ancient form of fortune-telling:

Draw a chalk ring on the table or tablecloth. Three new dice and a new cup or shaker box are needed. All three dice must be shaken in the box, with the box held in the left hand.

If you throw all the dice outside this ring, ask no more, and, above all, steer clear of quarrels! One or two of the dice falling outside the ring indicates the same warning in a milder form. But the thrower, in this case, may throw again.

The following are the common interpretations of the sum total of the numbers on the faces that fall uppermost:

one (that is one dice with one point and two with blanks) says 'Nothing doing!'

two slight trouble, and rather a lack of good news. Nothing to worry about.

three good. Seize the chance that comes *today*. Your wish will be fulfilled, or a pleasing or happy event will take place.

four a disappointment; but it will turn out to be for the best.

five news of a death, but no surprise about the news.

six a marriage, news of which will surprise if not distress the thrower. Also a sign of the loss of a portion of wealth.

seven an omen of good luck. All will go well in the matter about which you are now anxious.

eight disagreeable news through the post. 'Sit tight'. Better news will follow.

nine this is a good throw. It is a sign of good happenings but with some touch of scandal. Success in love or reconciliation of a quarrel or disagreement could also occur.

ten uncertainty, but nothing worse. 'Wait till the clouds roll by.'

eleven danger of loss of money through treachery. This also indicates the illness of someone close.

twelve someone seeks to involve you in an intrigue. Refuse to grant favours that are asked of you. There is danger of you being made a cat's paw. Do not act without seeking advice from a friend.

thirteen warns you that an enemy seeks your downfall. Throw again, and if the number is higher, he or she will not succeed.

fourteen long voyaging but not yet. Your travels will prove profitable but not easily. Always have hope. This is also an indication of a new friendship to come.

fifteen some domestic trouble. Examine whether there are people making mischief in your home. Sort it out!

sixteen you are going to be lucky in a matter of which you are not hopeful. Tell no one of your gains for a week after you know of them. Sixteen also warns you not to think too much about money. Other important things are being neglected by you. You will not want for money ever, but it will not supply the need of friendship.

seventeen indicates something very good indeed, unearned, unsought, even undeserved. You may well be thankful when this comes. Perhaps a suggestion or proposal from a stranger.

eighteen this is the very best throw of all. It tells of a high destiny, great luck and happiness. But beware of inconstancy when your luck is at its highest. 'The full cup needs a steady hand.'

Fortune-telling by Dominoes

A unique accomplishment is to reveal the future using dominoes, and there is something sufficiently fascinating and mysterious about this method of fortune-telling to fill the uninitiated with awe at the powers of the exponent.

Each small oblong has its secret meaning by which some happening vital to the subject is illustrated. It is a simple matter to commit these to memory, and in this, as in other methods of fortune-telling, the fundamental principle is that of comparison and calculation.

The dominoes used range from double-six to double-blank, and these symbolize the various conditions of fate likely to befall mankind. The exponent places the dominoes on the table and, having turned them face down, proceeds to shuffle them. When this is done, the subject is requested to draw three pieces, one at a time. Between the choice of each, the dominoes should be shuffled.

The first supplies an impression. If it is drawn a second time, the impression becomes a conviction. The third, however, may lessen or wholly contradict its degree of importance, and this is where calculation and comparison in blending the signs are essential.

Do not draw more than three pieces at a single consultation, or, indeed, on the same day or you may well find that interpretations are misleading.

double-six an emblem of matrimonial happiness and financial prosperity.

six-five almost equally fortunate—perseverance and concentration are rewarded by ultimate success.

six-four a comfortable income and happiness in marriage.

six-three fate smiles on love and marriage of the subject.

six-two prudence, hard work and a certain amount of good luck, or exposure and shame for any wrongdoing.

six-one two marriages to a young subject, the first of which will not be as happy as the second. If the subject is middle-aged, it foretells the speedy arrival of good things and the fact that he or she will never be lonely and uncared for.

six-blank unfortunately, a sign of great trouble—sickness, death or heavy money losses.

double-five all achievements will be rewarded with great success but inordinate wealth is not prophesied.

five-four almost as unfortunate as six-blank. If a girl lifts it, it means that her future husband will be poor and leave her a widow. Further, he may be of an extravagant disposition in spite of his poverty.

five-three a tranquil and contented existence. Sufficient money and matrimonial affection of moderate strength, the couple being incapable of passionate devotion.

five-two a warning that love and marriage are destined to an unhappy termination.

five-one social popularity but financial worries and losses.

five-blank a demonstration of egotistical and avaricious characteristics, tendencies to swindling and intrigues. It is also a warning to remain unmarried.

double-four the person who earns a livelihood by manual labour may regard this domino as a sign of future security and prosperity, but to those whose profession needs mental achievement it is rather disastrous. Troubles and disappointments await.

four-three matrimony and moderate income.

four-two an early marriage and moderate income.

four-one wealth or many friends.

four-blank a sure warning that single life will be the best and happiest. It counsels that any secrets imparted to another will be indiscreetly revealed.

double-three enormous riches.

three-two prosperity in matrimony, travels and speculations.

three-one some danger and unhappiness. The necessity for acting with extreme caution in all matters.

three-blank domestic unhappiness—such as a quarrel or incompatibility of temperament of husband and wife. Absence of harmony in the home.

double-two average happiness and income.

two-one two marriages, if the individual is a woman; financial failures to a business person.

two-blank the intrigues of unscrupulous people will meet with temporary success. It also denotes poverty and an indolent husband. The individual will return safely from all journeys undertaken.

double-one an existence free from money worries; peace and constancy in love and marriage.

double-blank the deeds of unprincipled people seem to be favoured; lack of integrity in a lover or husband.

Fortune-telling by Numbers

We all have 'lucky numbers'—but what are they and where did they come from? Numbers have a major part to play in our lives. They are everywhere. There are quite simple ways of identifying the special number that brings you luck on a certain day.

That a certain amount of character and fortune may be revealed by means of figures is a fact that can be tested for itself. The results achieved by this method of fortune-telling can be very rewarding to the mathematician in the attempt to solve the riddle of human nature.

Certain groups of figures stand for different qualities. Those given in the table below are only a small portion of the whole, but they are sufficient for the beginner. Each letter of the alphabet has its accompanying digit, and each digit has its abstract condition:

A 1 passion, ambition, design
B 2 destruction, death
C 3 religion, destiny, the soul
D 4 solidity, sagacity, power
E 5 the stars, happiness, graces, marriage
F 6 perfect labour
G 7 course of life, repose, liberty, success
H 8 justice, preservation
I 9 imperfection, grief, pain, expectation

J	600	perfection
K	10	success, reason, future happiness
L	20	austerity, sadness
M	30	fame, a wedding
N	40	fetes, a wedding
O	50	pardon, liberty
P	60	widowhood
Q	70	science, the graces
R	80	a cure
S	90	blindness, error, affliction
T	100	divine favour
U	200	irresolution
V	700	strength
W	1400	perfection of strength
X	300	safety, belief, philosophy
Y	400	long and wearisome journey
Z	500	holiness
	800	empire
	900	war, combats, struggles

The first thing to ask is the name of the subject. He or she writes it on a slip of paper and next to each letter its accompanying figure. Here is the name Dick James Smith:

D	4	J	600	S	90
I	9	A	1	M	30
C	3	M	30	I	9
K	10	E	5	T	100
		S	90	H	8

Now they are added separately:

    Dick = 26   James = 726   Smith = 237

Add the three totals together:

Dick	26
James	726
Smith	237
	989

The interpretation:

900	war, combats, struggles
80	a cure
9	imperfection, grief, pain, expectation,

the deduction being that he has a quarrelsome, headstrong nature, optimism and inefficient will-power, which are destined to cause him trouble, loss and misery.

Should the total of the names reach beyond 1390, the first digit must be subtracted, for example, as in the name Johannah Christine Whiting:

Johannah		Christine		Whiting	
J	600	C	3	W	1400
O	50	H	8	H	8
H	8	R	80	I	9
A	1	I	9	T	100
N	40	S	90	I	9
N	40	T	100	N	40
A	1	I	9	G	7
H	8	N	40		
		E	5		
	748		344		1573

Total = 2665, take away the first figure, leaves 665.

600	perfection
60	widowhood.
5	the stars, happiness, graces, marriage,

the analysis showing that Johannah Christine Whiting's life will be a mixture of joy and sorrow, the latter borne by a courageous and tranquil spirit. Her integrity and attractiveness of character will, no doubt, bring her much love and friends.

If the fortune-teller has a good memory, the table of qualities can be memorized, and a great aid to this is to practise with it, perhaps analysing an author, statesman or friend.

The fortune-teller's own name should reveal the fundamental truths of this method, and the analysis of people from history will show the distinguishing traits that have made them famous. For example, take Florence Nightingale:

F	6		N	40
L	20		I	9
O	50		G	7
R	80		H	8
E	5		T	100
N	40		I	9
C	3		N	40
E	5		G	7
			A	1
			L	20
			E	5
	209			246

Total = 455

400	long and wearisome voyage
50	pardon and liberty
5	the stars, happiness, graces.

The Numbers of the Alphabet

1	2	3	4	5	6	7	8	9
A	B	C	D	E	F	G	H	I
J	K	L	M	N	O	P	Q	R
S	T	U	V	W	X	Y	Z	

Now suppose your name is Gladys Templeton. Write it downwards, like this:

G — 7		T — 2
L — 3		E — 5
A — 1		M — 4
D — 4		P — 7
Y — 7		L — 3
S — 1		E — 5
		T — 2
		O — 6
		N — 5

Total = 62

You have added to each letter the number that stands for it. Their total value added together is 62. These two numbers add up to 8. You may bank on the importance of this 8, although there are some numerologists who would add to it certain mystic numbers that represent the day on which you make the calculation. The above is simple and it works out, strange to say, with striking results!

Finding your Lucky Number

Suppose you were born on 16 June 1971:

         Take the date of the month   = 16
         Add the figures together   1 + 6 = 7

June is the sixth month, so add   6
Add the year of your birth   1971
                                       1984
Add these figures together $(1 + 9 + 8 + 4) = 22$
and 22 (i.e. 2 and 2)   = 4

You will find that the figure 4 will turn out well for you;
also any figures or any number in which it appears or any
of its multiples (8, 12, 16) as well as 49, 48, 94, 84 and
especially 40, for the 0 intensifies any figure that it comes
after.

Note that number 4 itself is not a very good number,
although it will be favourable for you. People whose
number is 4 suffer from 'temper'—their own, as well as
those of other people. To live in a house that is number 4,
to get a bus or train or theatre ticket in which 4 appears,
especially if the whole adds up to 4 or to a multiple of 4—
this means happy travelling, auspicious enterprises.
Wednesday being the fourth day of the week, will be
lucky; April, the fourth month in the year also, especially
if these are the day or month of your birth.

But if you particularly dislike the number 4, it is up to
you to change it. Some people add the day of the week's
number to those given, Sunday being 1, Monday 2, and so
on. This plan, if you adopt it, gives you a different
number. You may work them both together, using one for
business and the other for personal luck. But do not
change entirely from 4 if it is serving you well.

Weather Fortunes

We often have a need or desire to know what weather can be anticipated—perhaps when planning a holiday or a wedding, or there may be an important sporting event where the weather will play a part. There are many signs to note.

Insects, Birds, and Animals as Weather Prophets

bats numerous at night, flying about longer than usual, indicate fine, warm weather the next day. Fewer bats than usual in the evening, or when bats seek to enter sheds and houses, indicates bad weather tomorrow.

owls crying indicates fine weather.

ravens croaking in the morning also predicts fine weather.

ducks and **geese** rushing here and there and diving into the water when the weather is fine, a storm is coming.

bees making short journeys from their hives, promise rain. The same applies when they come back in swarms before night and without being heavily laden.

pigeons returning late to the pigeon-house indicates rain the following day.

sparrows chittering freely and flocking together indicates that bad weather is near.

hens rolling freely in the dust and **cocks** crowing in the night are a sign that rain is coming.

swallows skimming the surface of the water or flying close to the ground tell of bad weather. But when they hawk very high, this indicates continued fine weather.

flies that are very restless and troublesome signal that a storm is coming.

gnats assembling before sunset into a circling mass are an indication of fine weather.

frogs croaking more than usual; **toads** coming out of their holes in great number; **worms** appearing on the surface of the soil; **moles** throwing up more earth than usual; and **oxen** and **turkeys** collecting together—all these signs foretell heavy rain.

cattle in the fields and **sheep** grazing particularly intently, say that rain is near. Cattle gathering together or remaining still grouped closely together tell that thunder is approaching.

cats licking their paws often and rubbing them over their faces, say that rain is near. The cat turning her back to the fire, tells of a storm. Cats with their tails up and seemingly electrified tell of windy weather coming. **Pigs** restless and grunting loudly also promise wind; for pigs are said to be able to see the wind.

Weather and Inanimate Things

rain may be expected when distant objects are seen more distinctly, or when they appear nearer than usual.

wind may be expected if the coals in an open fire flare higher than usual or flame actively. Wind, or some change in the weather, is likely when bells are heard from afar.

fair weather when the flames of the coals in an open fire
burn evenly and steadily.

frost when the flame is low and blue.

fine weather when the smoke goes straight up.

rain when it blows sideways as soon as it leaves the chimney.

rain when smells, pleasant or offensive, are stronger than
usual.

violent storms when the wind changes quickly and often.

rain or a **thaw** when salt, marble, iron, and glass become
moist, when the wood of doors and windows distends
and smells, and when corns on the feet become painful.

Weather and the Moon

*'A Saturday's moon
Comes it once in seven years—comes too soon.'*

A new moon on Sunday is still more unfortunate, while
if it comes in and goes out on a Sunday, we may expect
the worst in the way of weather.

'If you point at the moon, rain will surely come!'

If the moon lies on its back in its first quarter, it is holding all the rain there is in its lazy curve, and will tip the
whole lot out on earth when it straightens itself up. The
moon seems to tell of nothing else but rain. If it has a lead-
coloured ring, rain is promised. If the circle is red, wind
with rain. If its halo is small, rain; if large, rain. But if
there is no halo at all, then we can hope for fine weather.

Christmas Weather

*'A warm Christmas, a cold Easter.
A green Christmas, a white Easter.*

> *Christmas in snow, Easter in wind.*
> *A light Christmas, a heavy sheaf.'*

If there is wind on Christmas Day, there will be much fruit.

'So far as the sun shines on Christmas Day, so far will snow blow in May.'

If the sun shines through the apple tree on Christmas Day, there will be a good crop the following year.

Snow at Christmas brings a good hay crop for the farmer next year.

Strange Weather Coincidences

These appear to have been amply verified. 8 to 10 February are always cold days, however mild the weather has been up to then. 11 to 14 April, 9 to 14 May, and 30 June to 4 July are also consistently cold. 12 to 15 July, which is St Swithin's Day, are generally exceptionally hot. 1 to 8 August is a wet spell in nine years out of ten. 6 to 12 August are cold, followed by great heat.

The last few days of September are generally fine, and about 18 October we have, as a rule, a sweetly mild period known as 'St Luke's Summer'. 6 to 10 November are, as a rule, very cold; and December has a mild spell between the 3rd and the 8th.

The Months and their Fortune

January those who have a birthday in January are ambitious, proud, loyal, careless as to appearances. They are reserved and averse to showing their feelings. They have good business ability if born in the second half of the month. The men are interested in engineering.

The 3rd and 13th January are among the twenty-eight outstanding good days of the year. These dates are auspicious for everyone, although nobody ought to become engaged in this month.

January-born people should dress in browns, greys and black. They ought always to wear a garnet, which is the stone for their month, but it must be given to them with love and not bought. They marry most happily partners born either in February or in July.

February February-born people have good memories and are imitative and quick-witted; with acute understanding, although they are too apt to run away from 'stiff thinking'. They love dress and crave authority. They often suffer from rheumatic ailments.

They should wear purples, bluish-purples and black if born in the first part of the month. Those born in late February will find the red purples more lucky for them than the blues. They should always wear an amethyst. Those born in the first part will find 3 their lucky

number, but those born in the latter half may place their
dependence on number 9.

Tuesdays and Saturdays are good for the February-
born, and March is a good month for them to embark on
new enterprises. They live happily with partners born
either in January or in October.

March these people are generous, impressionable, easy-
going in money matters, apt to let good chances slip
past them. But they *can* fight when they are really up
against it, although they do not always, even then, keep
what they gain. Wearing the bloodstone, which is the
month-stone of March, ought to help the March-born to
cultivate that *steady* courage which they lack.

They may wear all-greens and will look well and feel
happy when dressed in green and red together. Good
days for the March-born are the 3rd, 22nd and 30th. Fri-
days in their own month are propitious for them to embark on voyages or enterprises. March people are rarely
very strong, although they are healthy.

March engagements do not last as a rule. And March
people find happiness with those born either in September or in July.

April the April-born are headstrong, erratic, fond of being
in the limelight, fickle. Over-easily 'up' and too soon
'down' as regards their spirits. But they make good
travellers, for they love change and despise the com-
monplace and the ordinary.

They do not think things out, but they can, and do, advise others wisely. All too often they complicate their
own lives and are unfortunate in their relationships with

people in general, in spite of being very sympathetic.

They ought to dress in blues, greys, greens and reds; but for evening wear, even when elderly, white is their most lucky wear. They should make important changes in April, and wear their own stone always, this being the diamond.

They should marry someone they have known for years (hasty marriages are never good for the April-born) and should choose their life partners from those born either in July, August or September.

May May-born people are vivid, hopeful and eager for adventure. They are somewhat obstinate yet neither persevering nor patient; affectionate but not generous. Destiny plays a big part in their lives; it is the unexpected that happens to them. They are fascinating, with a flair for dress and a real talent for art in any of its manifestations. They do not easily learn by experience, yet they do not worry.

They ought to dress in vivid emerald green as much as possible, and wear their own emerald always. Good days are 4th and 20th May—these are for everyone. Good days for the May-born are the 4th, 22nd and 28th. The 9th of June is very auspicious for May people, and they should marry partners born in May or June, although the May-born join confidently and successfully with partners born in any month in the year.

June those who have birthdays in this lovely month are 'born rovers'—travellers, adventurers and pioneers, loving to wander far from the land of their birth. They are restless, magnetic, impetuous, apt to act on impulse, eloquent, dramatic, nervous, and, if born before the 20th of the month, inclined to be dreamers and even workshy. They influence other people but are not easily influenced themselves.

June is a favourable marriage month for anyone. These dates are good for everyone—5th, 13th, 17th, 26th, 28th and 29th. The 3rd and the 8th are especially good for June-born people to start new ventures.

Those born in June should dress in soft shades of red and yellow, and especially in white, and wear an agate on the third finger of their left hands, for this is said to give them the power to attract to themselves the love of anyone on whom they set their hearts. They marry most happily with people born either in November or December.

July July-born people are generous and big-hearted, but they are over-anxious for pleasure and crave wealth, power and authority. They are patient, persevering and very thorough in all they do. They are not helpful in emergencies, for they require time in which to think things out. They never neglect appearances.

July-born people often have a hard time in their youth. They are great workers and also lovers of music of every description. They ought to take care of their lungs and check their love for flattery. They may dress in all the colours of the roses (never in blue, for who ever saw a blue rose?) and wear a ruby all the time. Mondays and Thursdays through the year are favourable days for them, especially for love.

Good dates in this month are the 5th, 6th, 15th. The

15th and 18th of July are particularly good for the July-born. They are happy with partners born either in January or in March.

August August-born people are steadfast and truthful, but vindictive when really vexed. Their strong sense of family leads them to shoulder burdens that do not properly belong to them, and they are all too often imposed on by the selfish and the lazy. This fact makes them become oversuspicious in later life.

They ought to dress in greys, drabs and all the shades of tomato red, also deep yellows. They must take special care of their eyes and wear a sardonyx, which is their own stone. An August woman rarely marries her first love, nor does an August-born man either. They are old for their years and are most successful with partners older than themselves, preferably those born in May or December.

The 18th of August is a good day for everybody. The first Monday in this month is a day of evil omen.

September those born in September are full of nervous force, talented, but not really practical, with a special gift for languages. They are serious, sympathetic and warmly affectionate but not especially devoted, for their weakness is laziness, and they are over-disposed to be easily sorry for themselves. As middle age approaches they may be tempted to intemperance.

July is lucky for them, especially for travelling. The numbers 5 and 6 will serve them well. The 4th, 7th, 9th, 17th, 28th and 30th of September are good days for everyone. Those born in the first week in September should wear primrose, in the second week violet, in the third and fourth weeks pale greens. But September people are generally happy when wearing blues, violets and primrose yellow.

Their stone is the sapphire. They should choose a partner born either in March or January.

October October-born people are equable, sensible, fond of knowledge but always practical and willing to use what they know to their own advantage. Those born in the first half lack ambition, those born after the 22nd are more ambitious and capable of more patient work.

They are unwise in money matters. They dislike manual work, are averse to travelling, and they like to 'go easy'. They are constant in love and friendship but apt to dominate those they love. October people are successful when working on the land and will do well to acquire land of their own as they grow older.

The opal is the stone for October people. Unlucky for others, it is lucky for them, and its wearer may always count on keeping the love of those whose love they have won so long as they wear this beautiful stone with confidence in its power.

January is a good month for October people. The 4th and 15th of October are good days for everybody. Number 6 is lucky for the October-born, although number 5 is still more so for those born in the earlier half of the month. October people always look well when dressed in greys and dark blues, for these are the colours of their stone; but reds and red mauves and pinky reds will also induce a woman to feel happy, es-

pecially in the evening. Their life partners should preferably be born in February or March, or July or August.

November the November-born are reckless, extravagant,
discontented; riotously happy or miserably depressed,
fond of adventure, fond of spending as well as fond of
giving, fond of luxury, of the good things of the table,
and of 'high-life' generally. They are clever and far-see-
ing in worldly affairs and are only unwise when they
love.

They ought not to marry too early nor too 'easily'. November people are 'great givers' both in love and
friendship. When happily married, which is rare for the
November-born, they make devoted wives and husbands, but are over-strict parents.

They should dress in yellow, with shades of golden
brown, for these are the colours of their birthday stone,
the glorious topaz. They ought to live on plain food and
'stick to hard work and cold water'. June is the best
month for November people, and Friday is their best
day. Lucky days for them in love matters are Wednes-
days and Saturdays. Good days in November, especially
for those born in this month, are the 6th, 9th, 15th and
23rd.

Since marriage either makes or mars the passionate
November-born, their partners ought not to be much
older nor yet far younger than they are; and they should,
if possible, be persons born in October or in June.

December those born in December put business before
love, especially as they get older. They do not easily
forgive any wound to their self-esteem, and should re-

solve to think generously as well as to act generously. They are not very strong and, as they look well, they do not get much sympathy in illness. December people do not easily recover from ill-health.

December women are too apt to get into a rut and to stay there. They love to help, to give and to advise others. October is always a lucky month for December-born people, and Tuesday is their best day. They should marry either on a Tuesday or a Friday. New enterprises entered into on either the 5th, 6th, 9th, 17th, 23rd, 25th or 28th will turn out well.

The 31st of December is the only 'bad day' in this month. December people ought to dress in light blues and pinks; to see that they do not overtax their strength; and always to wear a turquoise, which will turn faintly green when a word of warning as to their health is needed. This stone appeases hate between those who once were friends and brings together lovers who have quarrelled. December people should marry those born in June.

Fortune-telling by the Cards

The qualities required to read the cards successfully are a good memory, a fine sense of the meaning of words, absolute sincerity and a wholehearted sympathy with the person whose cards you are reading (here called the subject).

A sense of the meaning of words is valuable in order to relate the cards properly. The good card-reader will not say '*very* lucky' when he or she only means 'lucky', nor say '*extremely* dangerous' when 'very dangerous' is sufficiently emphatic.

Sincerity demands that the card-reader empty his or her mind of all thoughts, except those required to explain each card correctly and to relate its message with those of the cards around it, which will confirm or modify its meaning. Sincerity insists that the card-reader must be entirely *selfless.*

Sincerity and Sympathy

Sympathy, which is *love*, ensures that the card-reader never tells anything that is bad except as a warning to the subject. Thus—'avoid that person', 'do not keep this engagement', 'do not let yourself get entangled with these matters or with those people'.

Sincerity and sympathy are not incompatible. Cards can tell only what is known, although neither the subject nor the card-reader may actually be aware of it. Things are already sure to happen in the future because of something that has been said, done or that has happened in the past; or because of something that is now happening although we may have no knowledge of it.

Note that the truth and usefulness of fortune-telling by cards depends on the intelligence, sincerity and sympathy of the subject also. The subject who gives concentration, honesty and love equal to that of the card-reader, will be guided and helped.

The Picture Cards
Kings are men of weight—older men.
Queens are women and girls.
Jacks are young, unmarried men.

The Suits
Spades stand for very dark people; clubs for dark or brown-eyed people, and hearts for all who are neither fair nor dark—those with dark hair and blue or grey eyes, chestnut-coloured people and warm blondes, with eyes that range from the darkest blue to coldest agate grey. These are the largest class, the people called 'between colours'. Diamonds stand for the very fair, the 'lint-white' people, for the red-haired, and for those who are quite silvery white.

The subject must identify each picture card, after choosing 'herself' or 'himself', according to sex and colouring.

But these picture cards (or court cards) have additional

meanings in certain combinations and under certain conditions.

It is only necessary for the present to realize that spades represent trouble, anxieties, sorrows and changes that cannot be helped or hindered. Clubs mean success that has been earned or deserved. Hearts mean love, affection, company, socializing, and diamonds stand for money, business and financial affairs in general.

Diamonds and spades are 'chancy' suits; they stand for *fated* things, whether good or bad. Hearts represent things that can be altered by goodwill and sympathy. Clubs correspond to matters that, with some effort, may well be changed for the better.

The Cards Reversed

Some cards have a right way up and a reversed way. However, this is only the case with sevens and some odd numbers according to the way the centre 'pip' stands, and with all the cards when they are turned over if the design on the back has a right way up. Many designs are so ornate and intricately patterned that no difference can be seen, whichever way the cards come into your hand.

It is, therefore, wise to put 'R' on the top left-hand corner of each card after turning the pack the wrong way up, if you can. (It depends on the design on the back; otherwise you devise your own 'reversed' way, excepting the sevens.)

The meaning of each card is considerably modified if and when it is 'reversed'. In some cases it is altered entirely.

Some card-readers do not recognize different meanings

in the cards when they are reversed, but the card-reader who wants to tell of subtle shades of meanings will do so from the first.

The Meaning of the Cards

Diamonds

Ace: a ring; paper money. *Reversed:* a letter about money or containing money.

King: a fair or white-haired man. *Reversed:* a treacherous man.

Queen: a fair girl or woman with white hair. *Reversed:* a coquette, or flirt.

Jack: a fair youth. *Reversed:* a selfish relative, man or woman.

Ten: money. *Reversed:* a journey concerning money.

Nine: sharp instruments; anger. *Reversed:* operation. With spades: loss by death.

Eight: short journey; roadway; walk. *Reversed:* small money; a gain that will not last.

Seven: child or pet. *Reversed:* disappointing money.

Six: hope. *Reversed:* trouble with subordinates.

Five: gold, riches. *Reversed:* the law; proceedings.

Four: society. *Reversed:* happiness.

Three: trade. *Reversed:* separation.

Two: fortune, sum of money. *Reversed:* surprise.

Hearts

Ace: the house; between king and queen, a love letter. *Reversed:* change of residence.

King: a man 'between colours'. *Reversed:* a fickle, inconstant man.

Queen: a woman 'between colours'. *Reversed:* a vengeful woman.

Jack: a lover or one beloved. *Reversed:* the best-beloved of the subject.

Ten: great affection; happiness; corrects bad cards. *Reversed:* change; birth.

Nine: success; desires fulfilled; the *wish card*: *Reversed:* love.

Eight: love and marriage; happy spending. *Reversed:* jealousy of men.

Seven: inconstancy; small success. *Reversed:* jealousy of women.

Six: the past. *Reversed:* the future.

Five: marriage. *Reversed:* arrival.

Four: a messenger. *Reversed:* discontent.

Three: success; near spades, insecure; near diamonds, with money; near hearts, with love; near clubs, with ambition. *Reversed:* opposition to plans.

Two: love. *Reversed:* opposition to love.

Spades

Ace: business; high building. *Reversed:* death; annoyance.

King: very dark elderly man or a man handling important affairs. *Reversed:* an enemy.

Queen: a dark lady; a widow. *Reversed:* plots and scandal. With her jack, a dangerous woman.

Jack: a very dark young man. *Reversed:* night; shadow; medical matters.

Ten: distance; across water; voyages. *Reversed:* sickness; trouble. With eight of hearts, bereavement.

Nine: failure; loss; undoing. *Reversed:* death (corrected by good cards around it).

Eight: night; illness. *Reversed:* deceit; plots; between king and queen, a separation.

Seven: determination; change. *Reversed:* accident; upset. With diamonds, most disappointing to present hopes.

Six: a voyage. *Reversed:* a surprise.

Five: mourning. *Reversed:* a loss.

Four: solitude. *Reversed:* a proposal.

Three: a quarrel. *Reversed:* confusion.

Two: a friend. *Reversed:* an enemy, once a friend.

Clubs

Ace: letters; papers; good documents. *Reversed:* delayed letters; unpleasant news.

King: a brown-eyed man; a good friend. *Reversed:* worried or perplexed man.

Queen: a brown-eyed woman. *Reversed:* a disappointed woman; sad.

Jack: a dark-eyed young man. *Reversed:* the thoughts of the subject.

Ten: a journey. *Reversed:* going across water.

Nine: a will or a legacy. *Reversed:* a troubled journey; delays.

Eight: affection of a 'club' man; good friend; ally. *Reversed:* papers; documents.

Seven: victory. *Reversed:* financial worry; delayed success or achievement.

Six: presents. Gifts. *Reversed:* ambition.

Five: a lover. *Reversed:* flirtation.

Four: pleasure. *Reversed:* delays.

Three: economy (keep your money!). *Reversed:* position; honour.

Two: children. *Reversed:* letters.

Certain combinations may now be learned with these meanings or they may be left until later on, when the student has mastered simple card-reading. However, the brief meanings given above must be mastered before any 'reading' is attempted.

Certain Combinations

A card 'with' one or two other cards means that both or all three cards come out in the 'set-out' by either of the methods explained on pages 60–65.

king of hearts with *nine of hearts*: a happy love.

king of hearts with *ten of hearts*: sincere love.

jack of hearts with *ten of hearts*: an ardent sweetheart.

jack of hearts with *nine of hearts*: an engagement.

eight of hearts between *court cards*: helpful friends.

ten of hearts with *ace of spades*: a birth.

ace of diamonds with *eight of hearts*: an engagement ring.

two *black tens*: a long voyage.

king of clubs with *ten of hearts*: true love of friends.

jack of diamonds with *ten of spades*: trouble and unrest.

ace of diamonds with *ten of hearts*: a wedding.

court card with *seven of spades*: treachery of a friend.

diamond court card with *nine of clubs*: a rival in love.

jack of spades with *nine of diamonds*: a physician.

jack of spades with *nine of clubs*: a lawyer.

ace of spades with *nine of hearts*: fulfilled longings (of the senses).

ace of spades with *nine of clubs*: a theatre, a place of public entertainment.

ace of spades touching a *queen* with the *eight of spades* near: illicit meetings.

Duplicates of the Same Card

Kings

Four kings:	honours; dignities. *Reversed:* litigation.
Three kings:	successful undertakings. *Reversed:* new projects.
Two kings:	friends in business. *Reversed:* new projects.

Queens

Four queens:	quarrels; scandal. *Reversed:* frivolity.
Three queens:	society; convention. *Reversed:* scandal; gossip.
Two queens:	friendly consultations. *Reversed:* gossip.

Jacks

Four jacks:	treachery. *Reversed:* a law court.
Three jacks:	disputes; affronts. *Reversed:* indifference.
Two jacks:	a bill; a demand. *Reversed:* false friends; treachery.

Tens

Four tens:	success. *Reversed:* an unpleasant surprise.
Three tens:	A happy future. *Reversed:* loss.

Two tens: A lucky surprise. *Reversed:* excesses.

Nines
Four nines: robbery; imposition. *Reversed:* avarice;
                extreme greed.
Three nines: delay to projects. *Reversed:* greed of gain.
Two nines: (red) riches; (black) disappointment. *Reversed:* loss.

Eights
Four eights: successful projects. *Reversed:* disappointment; failure.
Three eights: thoughts of marriage. *Reversed:* amusement; frivolity; flirtations.
Two eights: uncertain plans. *Reversed:* an undertaking, commitment.

Sevens
Four sevens: children. *Reversed:* intrigues.
Three sevens: upset; disturbance. *Reversed:* domestic worries.
Two sevens: a proposal. *Reversed:* worries.

Note that satisfactory card-reading can be accomplished by some methods without using the smaller cards. The sixes, fives, fours, threes and twos mostly stand for ideas. Their use belongs to more difficult divination by cards.

Sixes
Four sixes: ambition. *Reversed:* wisdom.
Three sixes: generosity. *Reversed:* wealth.
Two sixes: gain. *Reversed:* joy.

Fives

Four fives:	caution. *Reversed:* caution against unfaithful allies.
Three fives:	power. *Reversed:* wealth.
Two fives:	anxiety. *Reversed:* speed.

Fours

Four fours:	pleasure. *Reversed:* cleverness.
Three fours:	catastrophe. *Reversed:* suspicion.
Two fours:	extravagance. *Reversed:* speculation.

Threes

Four threes:	strategy. *Reversed:* disappointment.
Three threes:	deception. *Reversed:* success
Two threes:	victory. *Reversed:* loss; obstacles; success delayed.

Twos

Four twos:	news. *Reversed:* indifference.
Three twos:	alarm. *Reversed:* treachery.
Two twos:	a small wish. *Reversed:* self-control.

The Cut

You may cut the cards on every occasion before beginning to comb out the cards that are to form the 'fortune' proper by dealing them according to either of the following methods:

To cut—shuffle the cards well and put them into three lots, face upwards. Red cards are 'bright' cards and are better than black cards. Two reds out of three cards are better than the other way about, that is, two black and one red. But remember that clubs are never bad. Although spades are not bad either, generally they are not a cheerful suit.

Read the meanings of the cards you have cut, reminding the subject (or yourself if you are telling your own fortune) that what is told by the cut may be in the distant future, and that *it may be avoided* if it is not good. The cut *is* true, yet it is not *sure* to come true! It has significance as a warning or a promise. But if the same cards reappear in the 'set-out' or 'fortune', then their early fulfilment is emphasized.

Two Simple Methods of Card-Reading

You may now begin to cut the cards for yourself, that is, to tell your own fortune; for this will give you proficiency in handling, in reading and in 'telling'. The first method makes use of all the cards in the pack.

Choose as 'yourself' a queen if you are a woman, a king if a married man, a jack if a single man. Choose the suit according to your complexion.

Shuffle the 52 cards well, and, if you are using a new pack, turn some of them about a few times, to get the 'reverse' meanings, if these want to come out.

Then deal the cards out one by one, saying as you turn each one up on the heap before you: 'king, queen, jack, ten, nine, eight, seven, six, five, four, three, two, one, heart'. (We give the hearts an extra chance in each of the thirteen chances because hearts are always good and human nature craves good news).

If a king of any suit comes out as you say 'king', put it out above the heap and begin again—'king, queen,' etc. If a queen comes out when you say 'queen,' a two when you say 'two,' an ace when you say 'one' or a heart when you say 'heart', always put the agreeing card out and always begin again, saying the list in order of value. You would have to begin again when you say 'heart' whether an agreeing card came out or not, for *heart* is the last of the line.

When you have gone through the pack, take up the cards that have been thrown out again. However, do not begin with 'king' unless the last card was in agreement with your call and was put above in the 'fortune'. If your last card thrown in the heap was a six, begin with 'five' when you commence to deal for the second time.

Repeat the deal a third time. That is, comb out the 'fortune' proper by three dealings of the cards that have not agreed with your calling of the list, the discarded cards.

The disadvantage of this first method is that you may get very few cards out. In that case, things are probably going very uneventfully with you. Tell yourself, 'Happy is the nation that has no history!'

Great or important events are not imminent, either, if you have quite a lot of cards of the smaller values, that is, the 'under sevens'. Dealings with people are rare if picture cards are absent or are few in the 'set-out'.

A lot of picture cards means company or that you are going to meet people, even if festivity is not implied. But you may expect small worries if the small cards are mostly dark ones, especially if spades predominate.

Spades are (roughly) anxieties, if not actual troubles. Hearts are love, company, visiting, the home and pleasure. Diamonds represent money and business matters. Clubs, although black, are good and stand for success, power and achievement. Spades and diamonds are 'chancy' suits. You cannot help or alter or avoid the things for which they stand; and a lot of diamonds, although they represent money, do not exactly mean money earned or money that you can increase. Hearts and clubs are happier, more pleasant suits.

If, however, 'you' (the card that stands for 'yourself') come out, you can control the indications in the 'set-out'; you *can* improve matters if there are a lot of spades in your 'fortunes', and you *can* increase the good promise of the hearts or clubs that have come out.

The nine of hearts is the best card in the pack; the nine of spades the worst. When this last is 'out' by this first method and 'you' are not out, you must just 'sit tight'; do not attempt to do things—if you do, your efforts will come to nothing. Remind yourself that the cards may tell a brighter tale in a day or two.

Now read the cards you have combed out—they may be three or they may be thirty-three—by this dealing of the whole pack three times. Keep in mind the simple meanings you have learned.

The Second Method
In this second method you use only the cards above the sixes, that is, the four aces, kings, queens, jacks, tens, nines, eights and sevens.

Shuffle the 32 cards and deal, counting each card you throw out thus, 'One, two, three, four, five, six'. Put the seventh card in a line above the heap of discarded cards. Count six again and throw them out, add the seventh card to the first above. Repeat until you have only four cards in your hand.

Count these and throw them out, pick up the discards again and go on, saying 'five, six, seven'; place this third one out above; count six and put the seven always in the line above the discarded cards. On this occasion your last card will be the seventh and should be placed in the line above. Then pick up the pile of discards and continue counting and placing the seventh card in the line above until you are left with three cards. Count these out and pick up the discards, counting out 'four, five, six'; the seventh card will be placed above and the rest of the pack set aside, leaving you with twelve cards for the fortune reading.

Notice whether it is the black or red cards that predominate. Read the combinations and then 'read the fortune'.

Do not read these twelve cards one by one, as in the first method. Count to the seventh and then count to the fourteenth, which will be the third from the first card at the left hand. Count on seven from this, and add its meaning to the seven further on, going back always to the beginning, or the first card at your left. Do this, getting six (double-card) meanings, as you end on the twelfth or last card in the 'set-out'.

If you want to get more from the reading, you may now couple the cards, reading the first and the twelfth, the second and the eleventh, the third and the tenth, and so on un-

til the last pair, the sixth and the seventh, have been read
in conjunction.

When you become more skilful, you may shuffle the
twenty smaller cards and add one of them to each of your
'couples'. But remember that these twelve cards are the
'fortune' proper and that the small cards are used only to
obtain further light on what the six 'pairs' tell you.

Note that this second method gives you more of a story
to tell, owing to the linking up of the meanings of two
cards every time.

You can get to be a *reliable* card-reader with constant
practice of these two easy methods.

Advanced Card Reading

You may stick to these two methods and extract all that is
to be got out of the cards, although there are very many
more systems. Some of these are very intricate indeed.

The secret of success, provided you are intelligent, sincere and sympathetic, is to know the meanings of the
cards in the very fullest sense.

Here are the more involved shades of meanings. However, first note that each of the 52 cards can be allotted to
each of the 52 weeks in the year.

You can get your 'luck of the week' by one single cut
of your cards. It is not necessarily 'bad luck' if you do not
cut 'the card of the week'. It means a deservedly successful week if you cut 'yourself', especially if you have clubs
with you, for then the success is *earned*.

But a really bright and shining success is indicated if
you cut 'the card of the week', as listed below.

It will prove advantageous to learn these meanings, and all the deeper possibilities, as given in this advanced style of card-reading. You will find yourself gaining a tremendous amount of knowledge if you use the methods you have already learned *after* you have memorized the meanings of the cards of each week in the year.

Note that the weeks of the year are not read always from Sunday to Saturday in this connection, but always according to what day New Year's Day falls on. Thus 'the week' may be from Tuesday to Monday if New Year's Day was on Tuesday; from Friday to Thursday, if 1 January was a Friday, and so on.

The Cards of the Weeks

'I' (1) is for the first week in January and is represented by the seven of hearts. The rest follow in sequence as in this list:

I (1)	seven of hearts
II (2)	king of clubs
III (3)	eight of diamonds
IV (4)	ace of hearts
V (5)	five of clubs
VI (6)	three of spades
VII (7)	nine of hearts
VIII (8)	two of clubs
IX (9)	queen of diamonds
X (10)	jack of spades
XI (11)	ten of clubs
XII (12)	four of diamonds
XIII (13)	two of spades

XIV (14)	nine of diamonds
XV (15)	king of hearts
XVI (16)	eight of spades
XVII (17)	six of clubs
XVIII (18)	seven of diamonds
XIX (19)	three of hearts
XX (20)	ten of spades
XXI (21)	jack of clubs
XXII (22)	ten of hearts
XXIII (23)	six of diamonds
XXIV (24)	queen of spades
XXV (25)	four of hearts
XXVI (26)	ace of clubs
XXVII (27)	king of diamonds
XXVIII (28)	five of spades
XXIX (29)	three of diamonds
XXX (30)	jack of hearts
XXXI (31)	queen of hearts
XXXII (32)	four of clubs
XXXIII (33)	ace of spades
XXXIV (34)	nine of clubs
XXXV (35)	five of hearts
XXXVI (36)	eight of clubs
XXXVII (37)	ten of diamonds
XXXVIII (38)	two of hearts
XXXIX (39)	six of spades
XL (40)	seven of clubs
XLI (41)	jack of diamonds
XLII (42)	four of spades
XLIII (43)	six of hearts

XLIV (44)	queen of clubs
XLV (45)	two of diamonds
XLVI (46)	nine of spades
XLVII (47)	ace of diamonds
XLVIII (48)	seven of spades
XLIX (49)	five of diamonds
L (50)	three of clubs
LI (51)	king of spades
LII (52)	eight of hearts

Note that the nine of hearts should come as near as possible to St Valentine's Day (14 February) and that the nine of spades properly belongs to the dreary month of November.

Another Simple Method

The subject should shuffle the thirty-two cards, leaving out the sixes, fives, fours, threes and twos, and cut them into three groups. Let the card-reader take up the first pack and ask the subject to pick out three cards. These are to stand for *the past*. The second group is then taken up, and the subject picks out five cards to represent *the present*. From the third group seven cards are picked to represent *the future*. These are read in the light of the meanings given.

Further light may be thrown on the cards selected if each of the three, five and seven cards respectively are covered by one of the cards of smaller value. However, it is to be remembered that the 'fortune' proper is read in the cards selected, which include only those from the sevens to the aces.

To Wish (by Cards)

Shall I get my wish?

Define the wish in your own mind; shuffle the cards, keeping the wish clearly before you.

Cut once, and note the card you cut.

Deal the whole pack into three lots or heaps.

Now take up each group and look for the card you cut. If it comes in the same lot as 'yourself', the answer is 'yes'. If it comes with 'yourself' *and* if the wish card, the nine of hearts, is in the same lot, then the answer is 'yes', with great success or joy. If the wish card comes between 'yourself' and the card you cut, you will get your wish with love.

If the wish card appears in the lot with 'yourself' but the card you cut is not in that group, this means you will not obtain what you actually wished for but probably something that is better for you.

If the nine of spades comes in the same group with the card you cut, *and* 'yourself' also, a great disappointment is in store for you, although you *do* obtain this wish.

If the nine of spades comes with the card you cut, and 'you' do not come in that group, you will not obtain what you want but rather will feel bitter disappointment.

You do *not* get your wish unless 'you' and the card you cut while wishing are in the same group; and if there are many cards between these two cards, so much time will elapse before the wish comes true.

The nearer these two cards are to each other when they are in the one lot, the sooner will the wish come true.

Note that something good involving a surprise is promised if the card you cut in order to know if you will get your wish by this method happens to be the 'card of the week'.

Involved Meanings
Now learn the more involved meanings of each card. Note that while some of these differ from the simple meanings you have learned already, they do not contradict them. When you can link both of them, you will be a really proficient card-reader.

Two of spades this card signifies a removal. If 'you' do not appear in the same 'set-out', you will hear of a friend whose removal will bring him or her nearer to you. It does not stand for a rich or very powerful friend. If reversed, it means that one you now call a friend will, before long, become your enemy. But this meaning of an enemy in the guise of a friend more properly belongs to the meanings of small cards—those below the sevens—when used to confirm or modify the meanings of the weightier cards— sevens and upwards—around them. Thus, this two of spades coming up against the king of hearts, a fairish or light-brown-haired-man—whom you can identify— shows he *is* your friend, though you may have been doubting him lately. The two, if reversed, indicates that this particular friend is failing you in some way.

   To hold two twos gives you a small wish. Take advantage of it at once, noting whether the next card you turn up is black or red. If red, the answer is 'yes'. But if the black card is a club it is not an unfavourable answer, though it stands for 'no'.

Note that cards of small value must always be interpreted in relation to the meanings of the weightier cards near them and that if cut they stand for comparatively insignificant happenings.

Three of spades this card tells of a quarrel, but if 'you' are out with it, it is a quarrel in which you have the advantage. You are going to turn what looks like failure into success at the last minute. People who do this are never 'down' for long, especially if they *resolve to hold* all they gain.

This three of spades near the ace of hearts speaks of quarrels at home; if near the ace of spades it tells of business disputes. Near a picture card, it signifies anger with someone of that significance. But these are not important or angry quarrels, just disputes, contradictions and foolish wrangling—irritation rather than passionate anger.

If reversed, this card tells of confusion, doubt and apprehension. Delay any important enterprise if this card is in your hand, for the affair will be hindered by distrust and insecurity.

Four of spades if you cut this card, be prepared for sickness or for trouble in some form. This is not a good card. Even with good cards on both sides of it when it comes out in the 'set-out', it foretells loneliness and sadness of the heart. (An infallible cure for this evil is to go out and do someone a good turn!)

If reversed, this four of spades speaks definitely of a sickbed. But if next to a court card of some other signification than 'yourself', the sickness will be for a person of that sex and colouring—yet it may be disastrous for you, in some way, that this person should be ill at this particular time.

Five of spades if you cut the five of spades you are thereby warned to correct your bad temper! This is emphasized still more if it comes out in your 'fortune'. You are jeopardizing your own interest by indulging either your anger, jealousy or spite, or even hatred, unjustifiably.

Heed the warning and question yourself honestly. You may find that your anger is undeserved or your jealousy unwarranted.

If the five of spades comes out reversed, you will certainly be surprised, and not pleasantly so. This surprise also refers to the matter in which your anger has been misleading you.

It may be that this ugly little card promises you *mourning*. This is one of the least happy of its meanings. Be warned in time, or you will mourn indeed.

Six of spades this card says you will take a voyage or a journey towards water sooner than you expect. It will not be a prosperous journey, nor one that you can make profitable. For spades, even when they are not bad, stand for fatalistic things.

When it comes out near to picture cards, the six of spades tells of a voyage or of travelling towards the sea, relating to some person or persons of the colour and sex indicated by the court card.

If reversed, this card warns you of a surprise in connection with a voyage or a place near water. It will not be a very unpleasant surprise, unless other spades are on either side of this six.

Seven of spades this card tells of a removal or change or upset, which you should avoid if possible. Spades are not a good suit, and sevens stand for displacement or some kind of change. If you cut this seven reversed, be very watchful over your tongue and temper, and look closely into the actions of all third parties concerning themselves with you and with one you love. For this card threatens the loss of one dear to you, with much trouble, if reversed—not a loss through death but by estrangement or interference or because of the hate, malice or jealousy of others.

It is never of good omen. If near the nine of diamonds, you will hear of an accident; with the nine of spades also near, the person who has been injured may die.

Eight of spades this card stands for the night and illness, but if it comes out with good cards around it, some extraordinary things may happen in the night, yet your safety will not be seriously threatened. Between a king and queen, this card foretells of a matrimonial separation; near but not separating them, a danger of trouble of this kind. Between two kings, this eight warns of the alienation of business friends. With the nine of diamonds, business trouble is still more clearly indicated.

If you have two eights in your fortune, or if you cut two eights in succession, you are advised to drop the idea of an illusion or dream, or project or ambition that attracts you at the present time. If you do not drop it, it will drop you or fail you painfully. This warning applies especially to a 'love dream'—that is, the hope of attracting to yourself the love of a certain person who has no thought of you in connection with love. Women in particular should accept this warning of the two eights if they wish to avoid rebuffs or slights that would hurt their feelings. However, a man should also heed the warning. If he is indulging in hopes that will not come to fruition, this warning may be valuable to him. The appearance of two eights between diamonds signifies a false dream of money gains.

Spades generally have a sad significance, although with good cards near, they may speak only of delays to the happy events promised by the other cards.

Nine of spades if you cut this card at any time, your luck is out. Do not try any new venture or tread any new ground until a week has passed. If you do, failure and disappointment will dog your footsteps.

If it lies between heart cards, this ill-omened nine of spades tells of failure sweetened by love. But if other spades flank the heart cards, it is illicit love and the end is evil! Between diamonds, this nine tells of poverty to be followed by riches. Between clubs, of disappointment to be followed by success.

Next to or near the nine of diamonds you will hear bad news of a death; next or near to the seven of diamonds then an accident, which may result in the death of the injured person.

Ten of spades this warns you of imminent unhappiness, grief, or sickness—perhaps of a mixture of all three evils!

If it comes in a 'set-out' with the five of spades before or after it, you are about to suffer a bereavement. With the jack of spades next to or near it when you have set out your cards, trouble or unrest is indicated. However, if it is held side by side with the other black ten, a voyage—not necessarily an unhappy voyage—is surely going to be taken. Note that the two black tens mean a really long journey overseas and not just a cruise.

With the nine of diamonds, illness, probably accompanied by an operation, is indicated. With the nine of spades flanking these, the sick person may be in considerable danger.

Jack of spades this is not a good card to cut unless you are a very dark unmarried man, when it stands for 'yourself' and tells you to press forward with your plans—you are sure to win.

With another jack it tells of deceit. Even if they are the two red jacks, two jacks represent deceit. Three jacks together forecast dishonesty, swindling, often 'big business' frauds. Be warned—if you are connected with people whom you suspect of being far 'too clever' in business, cut your ties with them before they tarnish your good name or your credit. If your own affairs are safe, you will hear of unscrupulous dealings in financial circles when these three jacks turn up together.

The jack of spades with the queen of spades, when both reversed, speaks of scandal. You will hear tell of domestic trouble among your married friends if you deal such a combination in your fortune.

If you cannot place a personal explanation on the jack of spades, it may stand for night. Thus, the king of hearts and the ten of spades (sickness) warn you of a dear friend taken ill during the night, when this jack is near them.

Queen of spades this card is generally taken to mean a very dark woman. However, if the card is reversed, it is taken to represent a malicious woman, one whom it is certainly not safe to trust. Alternatively it can signify a melancholy or bad-tempered person, either dark or fair. Be warned against such a woman, whatever her complexion, and say as little as possible when you are next in her company.

With her jack, this queen of spades promises scandal as well as plots. Either a married woman of your acquaintance is playing with fire, or a married man is pursuing some woman other than his wife. In either case this combination indicates that the parties are running a considerable risk of being discovered.

There is a significant danger of scandal to 'you' if these two cards of evil omen—the queen and jack of spades—are next or near to the picture card that signifies 'yourself'.

King of spades this card says you will hear of, or from, a public or government official—a man of affairs such as a banker, lawyer, stockbroker, head of a public department, or of a big firm, or perhaps a member of parliament.

If the card is reversed, he is either troubled, worried, angry or not so friendly to you as he was or as you believe him to be. Look to the cards next or near to him in order to know more about this important man and his connection with your affairs. If the king of spades is reversed and between diamonds, he is bothered about money; between hearts, about his domestic affairs—or yours, if the card signifying 'you' intervenes. The conjunction of hearts with spades stands for sensual pleasures. With clubs, this card reversed says that his ambition is slow in being rewarded; with other spades, disappointment or failure, or it may even be that death threatens him. This is certainly the case if the nine of spades touches him.

Ace of spades this card promises big business, especially if it subsequently appears with diamonds near it. If reversed, the ace of spades warns you that news of a death is coming to you. If it is next to the nine of diamonds, it tells of a death caused by an accident.

The ace of spades with hearts near implies sensual pleasures.

If this ace comes between hearts, you will be involved in a violent love affair. Next or near to the nine of clubs, you will go to a theatre. This ace of spades between a king and queen signifies an illicit union or unlawful connection.

The ace of spades means a high building, probably an office block, when you are reading a fortune that is mainly concerned with business matters. This is especially so when the ace of hearts is out also. The two aces will give you 'the home' and 'the office', but remember that two aces always mean new plans.

Two of diamonds this is one of the small cards that means a big thing. If you cut it, you will receive a considerable sum of money, and if it comes in your 'set-out', the money is as good as in your hands.

However, if reversed, with a court card near, its significance is: 'Do not keep your present engagement, whether it concerns money or love'—that is, the last engagement you made or the one you should otherwise keep within 24 hours of cutting this card. You will certainly be surprised or startled in the matter of this particular engagement, whether you keep it or not.

Three of diamonds this card says: 'Watch your domestic affairs'. If it comes out next to 'yourself', act with caution and prudence, for scandal is buzzing about you. This card says 'be discreet', or else it suggests that you should warn your partner to be more guarded as to his or her conduct.

If the unmarried cut this three of diamonds, it denotes that they will shortly be speaking with a friend, and quarrels concerning business or money or legal matters are likely to follow.

Four of diamonds this card indicates some kind of trouble through friends. The four of diamonds always stands for company, mixing with more people than usual, making new acquaintances. But this company is, as a rule, business or 'duty' company; it does not include socializing or celebration, although many hearts around this card would modify this last meaning. In this case, a business gathering *with* celebration is indicated. This does happen occasionally.

The four of diamonds has some kind of a warning of a

secret betrayed. Hear everything and say nothing when you are in company after having cut this card.

Next to a club, this card stands for a car—still with a warning!

Two fours together convey a hint that you should check extravagance. When reversed they point to speculation. They do not say 'cease to speculate', but only 'be careful'.

Three fours together are not a good omen. It indicates catastrophe of some sort. If you draw them, remember catastrophic events may still turn out well in the long run. Diamonds stand for things you cannot alter or help. Sit tight, keep your head cool, and cultivate the long view, if your fortune shows three fours or even if you should cut them one after the other. In this latter case, the meaning is a warning as to probable catastrophe.

Five of diamonds this card tells of a settlement with regard to a money matter with which you are concerned— not necessarily a large sum of money unless it appears with other and larger diamond cards, or with that important little money card, the two of diamonds. The settlement will be unexpected or you will have a surprise in connection with it.

In a set-out in which 'you' do not appear, the meaning is the same but the settlement is not so directly for 'you', unless the card signifying yourself has been first cut. If reversed, this card signifies the law or legal proceedings and the successful ending is delayed.

Six of diamonds this card, when cut, speaks of hope and promises pleasure. But if it should be reversed, it threatens trouble from people beneath you, if you are in business.

If it comes up reversed in your 'fortune' and next to a king or a queen, it says that the person denoted by the picture card will be widowed early in life.

The single man or woman who cuts it reversed, and finds it next or near to a picture card, will surely hear of the death of a dear friend's wife or husband—this will be an untimely death.

Seven of diamonds if you cut this card, you are thereby warned that friends—or some of those whom you look upon as friends—are speaking evil of you.

If the jack of hearts comes next to or near this card, you are going to hear of a birth. If the jack and the queen of spades are in the same fortune by cards as this seven, grave scandal is threatened.

The seven of diamonds is not a good card.

Eight of diamonds the eight of diamonds stands for remarriage. If you cut it, you are either going to receive attentions from a widower or to propose to a widow; or you are certain to hear of somebody making a second venture into matrimony.

Diamonds signify money. They also represent casual, haphazard, 'chancy' things. If you have made a deal involving money, this card promises success—but it is not a success 'you' can engineer or influence by any effort on your behalf. It speaks of hope but of *blind hope*. It gives no place to will or work.

If a spade is next to this card, beware of danger or accident. However, if it is a club, money and business are better. If it is a heart, friendship helps greatly, especially if it is a heart card of high significance.

Nine of diamonds this card foretells of unexpectedly good business, although it is business your skill cannot influence.

Yet the actual meaning of the nine of diamonds is anger, wounds, weapons; you must always read it in this connection if it appears in your fortune by cards. If next to, or near the nine of spades, you will hear of the death of a friend who has undergone an operation recently, or who has sustained an injury or accident.

Next to a queen, this card tells of a woman who will undergo an operation; with hearts near, it indicates that this will be successful. If near the ten of hearts, it tells of the safe birth of a child to a woman of the colouring of the queen, who has, nevertheless, been in some danger. If the nine of diamonds is cut near two black tens, the card tells of news of an operation on someone a great distance away. When the king of diamonds appears with it, he always represents a doctor. Similarly, the king of spades is a lawyer or banker in this connection.

With clubs near it, the nine of diamonds tells of anger over business matters, but they are not, otherwise, unfortunate business matters. With the ace of spades, a serious quarrel over business.

Ten of diamonds it is a very auspicious sign to cut this card. The ten of diamonds stands for money; a good round sum of money, although not the largest sum you can receive, in connection with any deal or business venture in which you are interested. The little two of diamonds means a larger sum still.

Two red tens together signify a lucky surprise in connection with money. But if both are reversed, you will be in touch with prosperous and charming people who are over-inclined to look on the wine when it is red. Resolve not to share in their excesses.

Jack of diamonds this card says you may look for important written communications.

For a very fair or red-headed bachelor to cut it, his luck is in—he may do big things, and these will undoubtedly turn out well, for this jack stands for 'himself'.

If next to another picture card, the sex and colouring of the sender of the weighty messages may be deduced.

The matter of the letter or communication may be read from adjacent cards. Hearts signify things social and of romantic attachment; spades, sickness or anxiety; diamonds, money; clubs stand for things that have been long desired and fought for.

Queen of diamonds this card signifies either a very fair or a red- or white-haired woman. If you are a fair girl, it is 'you', and it is always exceptionally lucky either to cut 'yourself' or to have the card of your own signification come out. It means that you can control any matter in which you are interested; that you may *act* this week without fear. If you are married, the king of diamonds is your husband, whatever colour your husband may actually be. If you are *not* a fair woman, this represents a good woman of that complexion unless she comes up with spades. If she is reversed, she is a flirt and is unreliable.

With the king of diamonds, this tells of a married couple; but if the nine of hearts is with them, you will hear of the engagement of this fair woman very shortly. Any diamond court card with the nine of clubs says you have a rival in love.

King of diamonds if you cut this card, you will certainly have reason to see a doctor or you will have some business with a medical person. The business does not necessarily signify anxiety—to cut a picture card always indicates friends; kings are generally powerful friends.

This king of diamonds stands for a very fair man, a red-haired man or a grey-headed one.

If reversed, he may be an enemy or a treacherous person. More frequently, an enemy in business. You see how true it is that diamonds are 'chancy' things. When they mean good fortunes, there is an element of uncertainty about it. Yet diamonds stand for the morning, and for youth and hope too. But these are uncertain and impermanent.

Ace of diamonds when this card is cut, it indicates that you can expect to receive money through the post: cheques, notes, etc. When reversed, it tells that a letter about money, perhaps containing news of money, is being delayed although it *is* coming to you. Next to a court card, the money comes from a person of the sex and colouring of the court card's meaning.

If the ace of diamonds is with the king and the nine of

hearts, it promises you the offer of a ring and says that you will make a prosperous marriage; of course that is if 'you' are also held in the hand. If 'you' are absent, the monied marriage is for the person indicated by the surrounding cards. Or it will be within your reach but you look on the opportunity with indifference.

Two of hearts a visit from a lover. If reversed, the opposition to a love affair; or, if with clubs, the opposition of those who love you to some project with which you want to push on.

A man or woman in business may expect someone who loves him or her to come to the home, office or place of work.

Three of hearts this card promises success, but if reversed you may be careful that your own imprudence in the past, in connection with seeking this change, does not cause you sorrow.

With another heart near it in your set-out of cards, the three of hearts tells of achievement. Next to a picture card, it predicts a kiss from a person of the sex and complexion shown by the court card.

Two threes side by side tell of victory in connection with some comparatively small matter about which you have been anxious. Two red threes indicate joy with the victory. But if one of the two threes is a black spade, there will be jealousy, which will take some of the pleasure from your triumph.

Four of hearts although this card means a messenger, it

stands for stubbornness in connection with a matter on which you will receive a message.

If next or near to 'yourself', you are being stubborn about some matter on which you are pushing to get your own way because it *is* your own way and not because it is the right way. Ask yourself if it would not be better to put your obstinacy aside and begin again?

If next or near to the card that signifies the person on whom you have fixed your affection, this person will be hard to win indeed. But hearts cannot carry a really bad meaning. The comparatively insignificant four of hearts may serve to convey a message, having some reference to stubbornness—a stubborn aim or a stubborn person rather than a really persevering one.

Five of hearts this card has to do with married love, but it promises that the subject will suffer through jealousy. If cut in the week to which it belongs, the five of hearts tells you that you are sure to receive a present before long. But if it comes out next to a ten of any suit, an invitation is promised.

Near a king and queen, you are going to be surprised by news of a marriage. If near diamonds, a good change in money matters is promised. If the five of hearts is near any clubs, you will reap the result of your efforts and of your perseverance in the past—the amount will be according to the number or dignity of the cards. As a general rule, though, cards of small value rarely promise big events or successes.

Six of hearts this card speaks of the reappearance in your life of an old lover or of someone who, long ago, paid you attention—this person will proceed to court you in earnest now. When reversed, this six of hearts tells of some attempt to trick you. It is not a villain who will try to do this but a rather good-hearted though distinctly 'tricky' person. We all know this type—people who would rather run crookedly than straight, even when to go straight would be less trouble! Look out for such a person and ignore any attempt he or she might make to rush you into a particular line of action.

Let 'masterly inactivity' be your motto. If properly carried out, you cannot be beaten while you practise this policy.

Seven of hearts this card tells us of something that is not lasting—a gain in money matters that will be fairly short-lived, or an increase in one's income that will not be as good as it first sounds. It may be a small success in connection with social affairs—something temporary. Look at the cards on each side to find out more about the matter.

If reversed, the seven of hearts tells of the jealousy of women. Again, the matter on which this jealousy turns must be interpreted from the cards that surround it. However, although they *may* refer to passion, hearts are never entirely bad.

Eight of hearts this card, which belongs to the last week in the dying year, tells of a mind at ease and of a good, friendly feeling surrounding you. The key-significance of this eight of hearts is *thoughts*—happy thinking, generous thinking; and this is indeed a good sign to close the pass-

ing year and with which to open the unknown days of the
New Year.

The eight of hearts has a further message of happy
spending, perhaps of buying new clothes, which will
please you. Next or near to the ace of diamonds, the
meaning is an engagement ring in the coming year, with
happy spending of money on furniture, dress, etc, in the
immediate time following on the engagement. Further, it
implies company, feasting, and so on.

Note that, while eight is the number of movement and
change, the good omen of the hearts is stronger than the
uncertainty indicated by the number. Happy changes, due
to love, are promised by the eight of hearts, whatever
week in the year it is cut or dealt in the set-out.

Nine of hearts this is the best card in the pack. It stands
first and foremost for love: happy love, success in love or
triumphant love. Therefore, it is fittingly associated with
the feast of St Valentine, the patron of true lovers. This
fateful date was celebrated long before it became the
name day of the gentle Christian saint. St Valentine's Day
is actually the old Roman feast of the *Lupercalia*, of the
goddess of fertility, of the blooming of life.

This nine of hearts also stands for success. If you cut it
in the first half of February, or if it is dealt to you, be sure
to 'wish on it' as you touch it. You will succeed in love, if
love is what you are keen on at the moment. Success with
money is indicated if diamonds are on either side when
you tell your fortune. Success in your ambitions is indicated if clubs are near this lucky card. With the jack of

hearts it denotes an engagement. With a king and queen of the same suit, a wedding. These combinations with the ace of hearts tell of an engagement or a wedding at your home. With the card that signifies 'you', the engagement or the wedding is for you. This card near the ace of hearts promises a celebration at your house.

Ten of hearts the ten of hearts promises domestic and family happiness—a good change if there has been recent anxiety in connection with social or financial matters. The ten of hearts neutralizes the effects of evil cards near it, and it strengthens and confirms good omens. This is its *general* meaning.

The ten of hearts has a more particular significance associated with pleasure, a place of amusement or a party. If a ten of hearts comes next to the ace of spades, you are going to a theatre; next to a king, to a dinner party; next to a queen, a formal evening function, if you are a man. If the ten of hearts is next to a queen, in a fortune by cards told for a woman, it tells her that she can expect to receive something very pleasant through the post. Between a queen and a king, the card signifies a happy event, an addition to the family, is foretold. Next to a queen, a very ardent lover; for a single man, a sweetheart who is young.

The ten of hearts promises *change*, but it is invariably a very good change that is indicated.

Jack of hearts this card speaks of love and the thoughts of the loved one, which are active about you.

The jack of hearts stands for one who is beloved, of either sex. It promises a young man or woman a speedy and happy engagement. If it is next or near to the nine of diamonds, it tells of a quarrel with the beloved; if next or near to the nine of spades, it speaks of misfortune to the loved one.

If those who are not concerned with love and lovemaking cut this card, or it comes out in their 'fortune', it promises them much joy through the natural affections of the heart, which belong to every age and time of life.

Queen of hearts it is very lucky indeed for a woman with warm golden or chestnut hair to cut this card, for it stands for 'herself' and promises her that she may safely embark on any enterprise with sure hopes of success. She may also accept any opportunity that presents itself.

When this card comes out as part of the fortune, it means that the subject will hear news of a woman of the colouring represented. If it appears next to the jack of hearts, there will be news of an engagement. If it is on one side of the nine of hearts, with the king on the other side, this indicates a happy marriage. The king and queen of any suit mean, for a business person, a partnership or agreement. The queen of hearts next to the ace of spades stands for an actress. If it is reversed, there will be news of a handsome but changeable woman rather than an affectionate woman, which the card represents when it is the right way up.

King of hearts this is an extraordinarily good card for anyone. If it should be cut for a married man of this colouring—fairish or light brown—there is scarcely anything he may not dare to do.

The king of hearts with the nine of hearts tells of an

engagement; with the ten of hearts, indicating a happy marriage.

Two kings together in your fortune by cards signify an important business meeting that is being held about this time and that will ultimately increase your financial prosperity. Two kings reversed say that new business ventures must be closely watched if they are to prove successful. (Remember, you can only read king as 'reversed' if you have put 'R' for reversed in the top left-hand corner.) If you do not specifically identify the king of hearts as a relative, friend or lover, its general meaning is of a good, loving man with a rather hasty temper. If reversed, this indicates that he is inclined to be fickle.

Note that the king of hearts must always stand for the husband of a married woman who is 'between colours', when her cards are being read, whatever colour her husband may be.

Ace of hearts the card stands for the house. If reversed, it stands for a change of residence, a holiday or merely 'a strange bed' for a night or two for the person whose cards are being read.

A keen businessman or woman may take the ace of hearts to mean the office.

A picture card near and facing towards the ace means that a person of the sex and colouring indicated by the picture is coming to your house; facing away from the ace, such a person is going away from the place. With the ace of spades near, the visit concerns business. The ten of hearts near this ace indicates a party or a celebration in your home. When the jack and nine of hearts are near, this indicates an engagement for someone in the home; the king with the ten promises a wedding. A red king with his queen also indicates a wedding; a black king and queen show a partnership. If these are spades, the business of the partnership will involve some anxiety.

The queen and jack of spades near the ace of hearts tell of scandalous conduct. Two kings in the same fortune as this card show an important business conference. Depending on how near they are to the ace, this will mean more success for the subject's domestic or professional interests.

Two of clubs this card stands for letters. Cards of small value—sixes and under—are not important, but the smallest cards have their meanings, and these should be read in conjunction with the cards that lie alongside. This card says you are going to handle important letters. With two kings the letters will be about a business meeting; with two queens, about committee meetings or other gatherings. With the ace of spades and the nine of clubs, letters about a theatre or a theatrical venture. But the letters decide nothing. This small card promises nothing definite.

Two twos together in a hand of cards warn you to exercise self-control in a matter that will soon be in progress. Three twos convey a hint of treachery, while four twos tell you to expect very striking developments concerning a matter, although small and unimportant enough in itself.

Three of clubs if you cut this card, your position with regard to some matter that had threatened it has been stabilized. But you will do well to practise economy, for you are not yet out of the woods nor quite secure in your holding or position or job. If this card comes out in a 'set-out' among pictures, you will hear of one of your friends making a second marriage late in life; a very prudent, worldly-wise 'look-to-the-future' sort of arrangement it will be. To identify the blushing elderly bride or bridegroom, look to the picture card next or near to this three.

Among reversed cards, this three of clubs stands for quarrelling about a post or worldly affairs—small and rather insignificant affairs, for the three is a small number. But clubs always stand for effort, success, 'getting there', and when they are reversed only delay is indicated.

Four of clubs this card promises pleasures, but only on a small or insignificant scale and with some relation to business. If reversed, the four of clubs speaks of delays to a pleasure already arranged, or perhaps of some little hitch in the arrangements. Next to a picture card in a 'set-out', this card promises a journey or a business deal, involving a car or cars, with a person of the sex and colouring indicated by the picture card.

To anyone involved in important business, this card says: 'Be prudent and you will succeed; but the success you gain will bring you satisfaction rather than a real increase in money.'

Five of clubs this card suggests a new lover. If the cards around it are of small value, an engagement or marriage with the stranger is not promised. If spades are near, guard yourself against treachery or deception from someone professing a regard for you.

A girl cutting it reversed may indeed walk warily. A
man who cuts this card will find that a woman whom he
looks upon as a friend has a wish to be something more—
she wants to tempt him from his present commitment.

If reversed and set between a king and queen of the
same suit, this card tells you of matrimonial reactions dis-
turbing married friends. But with good cards around, the
rift will not widen; they will 'kiss again with tears'.

Six of clubs this promises gifts. It bodes well for your
ambition, too, but with bad cards near, it warns *against*
someone who is soon to give you a valuable present.

If it is near the ace of diamonds in a young person's
hand, it tells of the gift of a ring. For older people the gift
may be a valuable present of something *round*—a bracelet, a belt, or an oval tie-band. Yet one should always read
of this present in connection with ambition or business.

Two sixes tell of gain, and even though they might be
reversed, they promise a joy of some kind.

Three sixes promise that you will soon be in touch with
a very generous person. If they come up with the card representing 'yourself', you are being very generous.

Seven of clubs this card is one of the best in the pack. It
stands for victory. If you are concerned as to the result of
any business, or affair or contest, you may confidently expect the very best.

If reversed, its meaning is not quite so good, the significance, then being financial worry; but note that this is
not loss or even disappointment, only worry; at worst, it is
delay, which causes the worry.

Clubs are always good in relation to business inquiries, although they do not mean things are easy to come by. This card promises no mere good luck but victory by your own efforts.

Eight of clubs this card promises you the help of a good friend or ally of the opposite sex to your own.

In the fortune of a business person, the eight of clubs, if there is a king or kings near it, may mean a new partner in business. However, when reversed it tells of a warning against speculation, a warning that a *real* friend has already given you.

If it comes near black cards or hearts, your new friend is a person either of dark or of light-brown complexion; with diamonds near, he or she will be fair or grey.

The eight of clubs is a happy sign for lovers in distress. It tells of the goodwill of a friend, able and willing to help. Reversed, it shows one not so powerful, though very willing to make the course of true love run more smoothly.

Nine of clubs this card tells you that you are going to hear of a legacy or of some business following the validation of a will. If it is cut reversed, it speaks of delayed and troubled journeys, generally after or connected with a death or a funeral.

With the jack of spades, business with a lawyer is promised. With either the king, queen or jack of diamonds, rivalry in love is sure to crop up.

To an unmarried man or woman, this card, if cut, says: 'Do not act against the wishes of your friends.' However, to the married and to all those who are concerned with business or with secret affairs, the contrary advice is indicated: 'Take no advice but your own and you will do well.'

Ten of clubs this is a very good card to cut if business affairs are engrossing you. It says: 'Stop worrying.' Things are going better than you fear. It does not promise a dramatically good change but a sure and certain improvement. 'The slow success is the sure success'—especially in business.

This card often foretells of a journey, concerned with good business rather than pleasure. With the other black ten, a voyage is certain, and successful if red cards are around these two black ones.

All clubs signify ambition, success that has been slow and difficult to come by, manhood, decisiveness, and the more masculine qualities of the mind.

Two tens indicate a change of trade. Two red tens say a lucky and surprising change concerning your business. Three tens stand for prosperity and the promise of a happy future.

Jack of clubs it is very lucky indeed to cut this card at any time. To a dark young girl, it promises a faithful lover and a marriage founded on true friendship and mutual esteem. To a dark young bachelor, it says: 'Go on as you are now doing. You are surely working towards success.' If an older, dark man cuts it, or if it comes in a fortune told him, this jack of clubs bids him follow out the thought that at present grips him; in short, to act on his own initiative. An older, married woman who cuts the jack of clubs will hear gratifying news of her son's success.

For those who are not of the dark-brown complexion of which clubs are the signification, this jack of clubs says that a friend is thinking about them and they will certainly hear of him—a hasty, big-hearted friend, not necessarily a man friend but a very true one of either sex.

If a brown-eyed person's fortune is being read, the card-reader may make the card that particular person's 'thoughts', and if carefully noting the cards around this one, will be able to tell much of the hopes, aspirations and ambitions, as distinct from the actual events in the subject's life, at the time.

Queen of clubs if you are a dark-eyed, brown-haired girl or woman, it is very lucky to cut this card, for it signifies 'yourself'. It says: 'Go in and win! Be bold, be bold, and evermore be bold!' You will surely come out on top, whatever tight corner you are in.

If you are a man of this colouring, the omen is lucky in regard to love. For whatever the colouring of the woman you love might be, this card stands for her—she is *your* queen, and she is thinking sweet thoughts of you. However, if reversed, you have offended her or she is unhappy; ensure that you rectify this situation as soon as possible.

King of clubs it is always lucky to cut this card because the clubs stand for successful efforts, and kings are powerful helpers.

The club picture cards signify good friends rather than lovers, unless you are a dark woman (queen of clubs). This card reversed means that your powerful friend is worried or hindered—not *quite* so powerful on your behalf. With spades near there is trouble between you. If a man holds it with the queen near, a powerful partnership is suggested; with the wish card (nine of hearts) near, this indicates great success throughout the year. If cut with the ten of hearts, then marriage with someone you now regard as a friend is indicated. This last applies to either a man or a woman.

Ace of clubs this card signifies important papers, written plans, shares, contracts, leases—lucky, successful papers, in fact, rather than mere letters. Good business letters *may* be indicated.

If reversed, this card means a delay to written prospects or a delay over signed papers, with perhaps some anxiety as to the outcome.

However, unless surrounded by spades, even if the ace is reversed, it does not necessarily mean unpleasant communications regarding business.

Clubs always refer to ability, merit and things that have been earned or deserved.

Palmistry

Palmistry is an ancient art, and some palmists justify its study as a form of learning and knowledge from a text from the Bible, in the Book of Job (37:7—'He sealeth up the hand of every man; that all men may know his work'). Certainly, it is known to have been understood in Egypt and, farther back still, among the Hindus.

Palmistry can take its place as a serious study producing reliable deductions if the student is earnest and intelligent. Here you will find the art of palmistry explained in its clearest and simplest form.

The Anatomy of the Hand

The human hand is made up of the metacarpal bones and the phalangeal bones. Between the hand and the bones of the forearm—the radius and ulna—are the eight carpal bones of the wrist, in two rows. Between the carpal bones and the fingers and thumb come the metacarpals. These are similar in shape to the phalangeals, or finger bones, but are longer and are contained in the muscular envelope of the palm. Jointed to the metacarpals at the knuckles are the bones of the phalanges in three rows, the bones tapering towards the fingertips.

The thumb has only two phalangeal bones, and these, like its metacarpal, are shorter than those of the fingers.

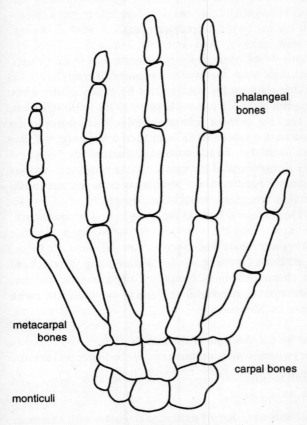

phalangeal
bones

metacarpal
bones

carpal bones

monticuli

The bones of the hand

The metacarpal of the thumb is capable of free movement, and it is this characteristic that makes the thumb an 'opposable' digit. Because of this we are able to grasp objects and use our hands in complex operations such as sewing, writing, drawing and working with tools. There are twenty-seven bones in the hand and wrist—eight carpals, five metacarpals and fourteen phalangeal bones.

One result of the hand's great flexibility is that while the palm is thickly padded in between the lines of flexion, or bending, at these lines the skin is bound down to the tendons that move the digits and to the deeper layers. This combination of loose and firm surfaces gives the necessary secureness and adaptability to the grasp. It is obvious that if the padding of the palm were loose and free to slip about, a firm grasp would be impossible.

The 'bracelet' lines at the wrist have a similar origin. The monticuli—the prominences that we see at the base of the thumb and fingers—are composed of muscle tissue, as are those on the phalanges. Nature has given the hand the characteristics of flexibility and firmness, and has cushioned the palm against shocks that would otherwise injure its framework.

The Size and Shape of the Hands

Large hands show order, method, obedience and detail.

Small hands show energy, government, ability to rule and executive power.

Medium-sized hands indicate a character with a capacity for turning his or her hand to anything. When the fingers are exactly as long as the palm, they belong to people who are successful in business but not in any highly specialized kind of business. Note that this hand belongs also to the 'Jack-of-all-trades'—the person who does many things capably but none of them exceedingly well.

Hands with palms long in comparison to the length of the fingers show an ability to make big plans, an ability to grasp things quickly and a dislike of detail.

Hands with the fingers relatively much longer than the palm cannot plan but they can 'finish' everything they do. A person with hands like these will not neglect or overlook the slightest detail. They are 'slow-but-sure' people.

Wide hands indicate kindness and sympathy—someone who is able to see and consider the other side as well as his or her own point of view.

Narrow hands belong to people who are critical and exacting by nature—those who see faults rather than good qualities. It is said that the best husbands and wives are not found with this kind of hand, but if the life partner's hand is too short and too wide, fate may draw them together

Hands wide open with the fingers well apart show originality, initiative and courage.

Hands with fingers close together show convention, fear of consequences and cowardice.

White hands show a selfish nature.

Red hands show passionate feeling, anger and energy.

Hands of warmish pink show a warm heart.

Soft hands indicate laziness, which may coexist with distinct and probably unused talent. But hands that are only moderately soft, or soft on the mounts, may belong to people who work best in short bursts only.

Very hard hands demonstrate energy and the love of work for its own sake. These are people who should ask themselves what it is that they want out of life and then set out to get it, cultivating mental disciplines so that they do not waste their nervous energy too extravagantly.

Square hands show reason, consistency, common sense and accuracy.

Pointed hands show spirituality, idealism.

Note that a hard and very square hand belongs to a person who always has reason on his or her side. He or she is never wrong.

The extremely 'peaky' hand—especially if it lacks 'grip' and feels unreal when it is grasped—belongs to the dreamer, the impractical person. With very pointed fingertips, these hands will have no sense of reality—they will take up and support the wildest notions. Tapering fingertips lack executive power.

There is a third hand, called the spatulate hand, which is the opposite of the pointed hand. It is rare and inclines to be distinctly ugly, with fingers that bulge at the top. This is the useful hand. Its owner is concerned only with material things, but this hand, when not excessively spatulate, belongs to the person of action—the worldly person. Its owner is practical, technically adept and would feel at home working with engines or machinery.

For a person to be an inventor or a really original thinker who can translate his or her thoughts into action, the hand must partake of all these three types, and every one of the fingertips must vary.

The mixed hand is the most difficult to read.

Palmists have over many years, defined seven well-marked types of hands:

> The Elemental
> The Spatulate or Active
> The Conical or Temperamental
> The Square or Utilitarian
> The Knotty or Philosophic
> The Pointed or Idealistic
> The Mixed

The Elemental Hand

This hand is the mark of primitive races. It is characteristic of peoples, such as the Laplanders, who inhabit Polar regions, and was also a feature of the Tartar and Slav races. The palm is large, and the fingers short and thick. Intrinsically the hand of the peasant or the serf of times long past, it is seen in all lands among those who for generations have come from the stock that furnishes the 'hewers of wood and drawers of water'. These people have, in the course of centuries, evolved as a type who have adapted to making a living by hard and rough labour.

Their acquisitive and self-preservative faculties have developed to predominance.

What significance is to be attached to the possession of an elemental hand in our subject? It depends, of course, on the degree of relation to the archetype, for the pure elemental is uncommon outside those regions that have been mentioned.

Superstitious, narrow-minded and unintellectual, this type has nevertheless produced, on occasion, great leaders—in religious persecutions and in the rare and dreadful peasant risings in European history.

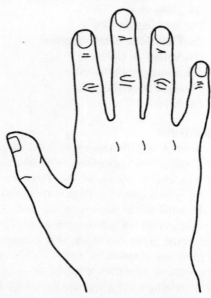

The Spatulate or Active Hand

This hand is large and broad, with blunt, thick fingers, broad at the tips. The digits are long. It is the mark of someone of action rather than a great thinker, of the tireless, restless agitator who seeks to improve the lot of others by his or her endeavours and adventure, of the bold and daring navigator of Polar seas, or of the courageous pioneer.

People with the spatulate hand have certainly played their part in history, in linking the Atlantic and the Pacific by railway, in cutting canals such as the Suez and the

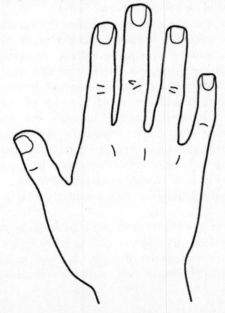

Panama, in opening up air routes across continents and oceans. They are generally intolerant of convention and original in thought and action. Women of the spatulate type are endowed with a large measure of intuition.

In games and athletics they may excel, and usually they are musical. Some of the greatest painters of all time have belonged to the spatulate type. In general, this hand denotes the executive rather than the administrator. Rulers of this group have made history by their failures rather than by their achievements.

The Conical or Temperamental Hand

This type of hand marks the emotional or temperamental subject—impetuous, impulsive and exuberant. The aesthetic perception is strongly developed, and beauty in all forms and guises appeals strongly to this person. Although scarcely artistic in the real sense of the term, he or she is sensitive to the emotional stimulus of music and pictures. A somewhat unstable nature is indicated—the temperament being coloured by varying moods that never endure long. Although generally cheerful and optimistic, this person is, however, easily depressed by any misfortune or by lack of success in trivial enterprises, and the mood of satisfaction may change suddenly to one of black despair.

The content of his or her mind is coloured by the conversation of any and every person he or she meets. Lacking skill in constructive thought, this type reflects the moods and opinions of those stronger surrounding personalities.

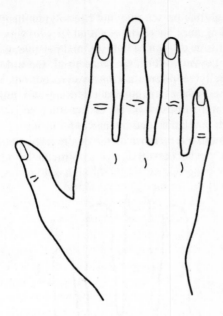

The wife or husband of this type is a somewhat difficult person. He or she does not easily tolerate discipline,
dislikes mundane routine, and craves for pleasure and excitement—for something new or different. Whilst hot-
tempered, this person is soon repentant after an outburst
of passion, and so avoids making enemies.

The Square or Utilitarian Hand
This type of hand denotes the methodical, matter-of-fact
individual, who is a steady, law-abiding member of soci-

ety. Although this person may not rise to great heights in intellectual matters, he or she is a plodder who very often reaps rewards as a result of industry and perseverance. In contrast to the owner of a spatulate hand, the utilitarian hand generally represents a conservative outlook and a sturdy support of the existing order of things—in religion, in politics and in business. He or she often responds to change with immediate and intense opposition.

A very valuable member of the community, he or she appears as the successful lawyer, politician or teacher who makes progress as much through self restraint as

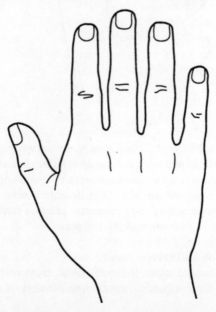

through good deeds. The owner of a utilitarian hand is a good soldier but a poor leader, because the utilitarian type is nonplussed when an opponent disregards the 'rules' or does something contrary to his or her own experience.

The man of this group makes a good match for a woman who is not passionately demanding. In matrimony, he is apt to take things too much for granted, frequently forgetting that his partner expects material, physical and emotional evidence of his love.

The Knotty or Philosophic Hand

This hand is noticeable for its bluntly conical fingertips, its large joints and its broad third phalanges. It denotes a materialistic type of mind: logical, methodical and systematic. This is the hand of the seeker of life's truths.

Such a person is inclined to be reserved and to appear 'standoffish'. This is quite undeserved; the reserve arises merely from a profound knowledge of and an interest in matters that only a few people will care to talk about. In the absence of people with similar interests, the philosophic appears aloof, but place him or her *en rapport* with a kindred spirit and the reserve vanishes. In the young person this temperament inevitably leads to a somewhat introspective tendency, and the subject is, generally, not a 'good mixer'.

A hard worker, the philosophic is honest with himself or herself as well as with others—philosophic types have few delusions about themselves, although they will always back their own opinions when they eventually arrive

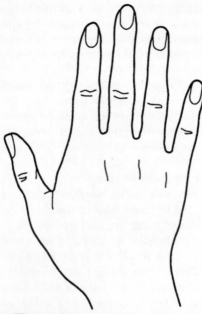

at them. They endeavour to keep an open mind during investigation or analysis of evidence. Although the philosophic may not be ideal as a choice of partner, he or she is generally a good parent, although just and stern. He or she may be sceptical about religion, but, nevertheless, might maintain a firm commitment to some creed.

The Pointed or Idealistic Hand
This hand marks the possessor as one who worships at the shrine of beauty—not material beauty so much as beauty

of the mind, although the artistic perception is usually well developed and the subject appreciates true beauty in everything. As a rule, the idealistic type is rather impractical in mundane matters, and has little idea of thrift or provision for future wants—like the grasshopper in the fable, who sings during the sunny hours but may starve in the winter of life.

Gifted with a vivid and creative imagination, people of this type love verse and literature; frequently they write, paint or compose. A marriage of two such persons is usually an ideally happy one, although the parties may have

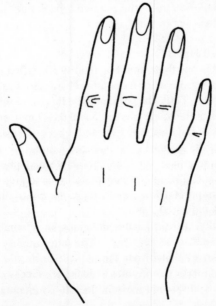

to suffer poverty. On the other hand, should the similarity of temperament be merely superficial, then intense unhappiness may result. Being naturally fickle and inconstant, idealistic types are in need of a very strong bond of love to hold them to their life partners.

This type finds much comfort in religious practices and good works. He or she worships wholeheartedly, and feels that beautiful music, pictures, lights, etc, fit in best with his or her idea of devotion. The less aesthetic side of religion holds less attraction for the idealistic type—theirs is not the stuff of which martyrs are made. We take an extreme case, of course—the pointed type is rare, and in its completeness is rarer still.

The Mixed Hand

This hand is one that cannot be readily classified in any of the other six groups, for it contains characteristics of some or all of them. Thus, the palm may be large and the fingers long, thick at the lower phalange and then tapering. It thus has points of the idealistic type and others that associate it more with the utilitarian. In another subject we may observe characteristics of both the active and philosophic types of hand. The rule of interpretation is to give value to the most important features. If these are contradictory an average is indicated.

Generally, a mixed hand indicates an adaptable temperament and some versatility. The latter quality may be so much in evidence that the subject turns out to be a 'Jack-of-all-trades' and fails to make a success of his or her life in consequence. Many brilliant engineers, inven-

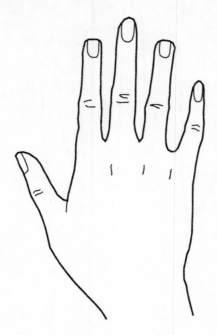

tors and research workers have belonged to this type, spending their life in pursuit of new technologies and developments. But when they have solved their problems they are not materially better off—although the world has profited from their discoveries.

The attributes indicated in a mixed hand are those of the types to which it is nearest in form. There are many varieties, and each must be analysed on its merits.

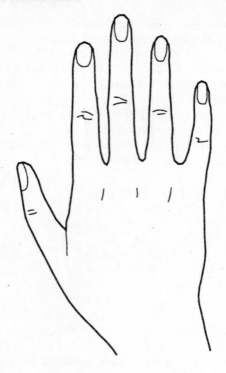

The Female Hand

Although the female hand, as well as the male, is classified in the seven types identified, the distinguishing features are not so strongly marked. A woman's hands are softer, smoother and more modelled, but the characteristics that have been highlighted can be identified.

The elemental hand is rare in women, and the spatulate and knotty types are less conspicuous than in the male. When any one of these three is found with strongly marked features, the attributes are present in large measure. As to the temperamental and idealistic, the interpreter may here fall into the error of over-valuation, for in many women the hand has something of these features without, however, belonging really to either type. The square or utilitarian type is more easily recognized, and the mixed type, too, can usually be distinguished.

The Fingers and the Mounts

The first or index finger is the finger of Jupiter. The second or middle finger is the finger of Saturn. The third or wedding-ring finger is the finger of Apollo. The fourth or little finger is the finger of Mercury.

The natural bend of the fingers is important, and the palmist should be quick to notice its natural attitude before examining the interior of the hand.

Some fingers are distinguished by their independent, prominent position over the rest. When the tips are inclined to curl to the palm, a plodding, determined nature is indicated—one that does not easily relinquish a set aim or purpose because of obstacles.

A wide space between Jupiter and Saturn shows unconventionality, and originality of thought and outlook.

When the Jupiter finger is upright and straight, and of normal length, a just, candid nature is revealed. Should its position be in advance of the other fingers, a respect for authority is indicated. If it falls slightly behind, this indi-

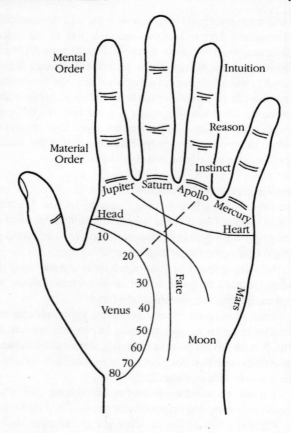

The human left hand as delineated for the
purposes of palmistry

cates dependency on others and a reluctance to take the initiative and the burden of responsibility. If the finger is short, this denotes ingratitude and no enthusiasm. If it is pointed, it is an indication of tact, comprehension and sympathy. A square finger is a sign of integrity, but also of someone who may be thoughtlessly frank in expressing opinions.

The generous and broad phalanges of Saturn show gravity, depth of character, and a sense of proportion. A short Saturn signifies imprudence and an inclination to act on impulse and to behave rashly— spatulate implies energy, and square indicates cool, clear-headed, thought before action and absence of hasty judgements.

If the finger of Apollo is well developed this shows artistic tendencies. If its position is slightly forward, the talent lies in painting, drawing or sculpture. A pointed finger is a sign that the artistic ability is greater than the practical. A spatulate shape shows a sense of the beautiful in form and colour, and possession of dramatic powers.

Mercury, set lower than the other fingers, reveals the fact that many adverse circumstances have been battled with. A pointed finger of Mercury indicates tact, discrimination and intuition. If it is square it shows a love of scientific pursuits and good reasoning powers.

The mounts under each bear the same names as the fingers above them. Thus we have the mounts of Jupiter, Saturn, Apollo and Mercury, as shown in the diagram on the opposite page.

The mount at the base of the thumb is the mount of Venus, and that opposite to it on the fleshy outer base of the hand, is the mount of Luna or of the moon. There are, in addition, two mounts of Mars situated respectively above the mount of Venus and below the mount of Jupiter; this is Mars positive. On the outer side of the hand, above the mount of Luna and below that of the mount of Mercury is situated Mars negative.

As the fingers and their supporting mounts represent the same qualities, it is easier to learn simultaneously what the fingers and mounts stand for. Note, however, that the finger in excess (that is, exceptionally long or large) stands for the nobler overdevelopment of the qualities, and the mounts in excess stand for their more fatalistic or baser overexpression. The hand is like the head in this respect. In the top part we read the intellectual qualities, and at the base the animal instincts.

Fingers that are weak or small and mounts that are quite flat, show absence of the qualities represented. Mounts that seem to be almost hollow—although this *may* be due to the very high development of the 'neighbouring' mount—indicate the qualities opposite to those for which the fingers stand.

Remember that in palmistry, as in almost everything else, *excess* is not a good thing. In real life the excess of any virtue may prove a vice! The wise ever seek to direct their actions in line with:

> '. . .the happy mean,
> A Vice at each side and the Virtue between.'

Thus, the excess of prudence is the vice of miserliness on one side, and its absence is prodigality on the other.

Jupiter

Jupiter stands for veneration, worship, religion. A very dominant first finger indicates the hands of great religious leaders and all those whose sense of honour is extremely high. With the mount big and out of proportion, then religious mania or enthusiasm run wild. If the mount is hard, fanaticism is indicated—if it is soft and high then the subject is said to be of a sympathetic nature but with strange beliefs.

Saturn

Saturn stands for knowledge, thought, occultism, superstition. This second mount, if unusually high, will denote fatalism, melancholy and esoteric knowledge. The subject will say—'I cannot do or undo. What must be, will be.'

When the second finger is big and square, this indicates a thoughtful but not a practical person—a pointed finger is a sign of unbalanced thought.

When Saturn's mount is flat, there is a total lack of imagination; and people without imagination are apt to be cruel. But this mount may appear flat because of the height of Apollo, which denotes joyousness as distinct from the sadness of Saturn.

Apollo

Apollo signifies art, beauty, wealth and joy in living.

This mount is highly developed in all artists who have an inborn love of colour and of beauty. But if the hand is soft, there may be an over-strong enjoyment of pleasure through the senses. If the mount of Apollo is flat, it illustrates a nature that detests joy and almost seems to dislike beauty and to dread happiness.

A long thin finger of Apollo indicates a love of colour, and if the thumb is strong there will be capacity to express this in some form of art.

Mercury

Mercury denotes persuasive speech, business and worldly shrewdness. If the mount is very high and the finger pointed, it indicates a person who is perhaps 'too clever' or even tricky, especially if Jupiter is poor. A crooked little finger indicates a thief, one who steals not because of need but because he or she likes to do so. The mount of Mercury, if very flat, shows an individual with no foresight and the inability to seize a chance when it presents itself. Mercury's finger, if square at the top, shows one who can both buy and sell to advantage.

So much for the mounts that distinctly belong to the fingers.

The Thumb

The possession of a thumb, a digit that can be placed in opposition to the fingers, differentiates human beings from all the animals except certain apes and monkeys. It is a most valuable addition, for humankind could never have developed without it. The ability to make and use crude and rough tools enabled our primitive ancestors to set out on the evolutionary path that has led to our civilization of today. From rough tools they could fashion finer and more efficient ones—first of flint, then of bronze and iron—and utilize them to build and construct. No wonder the thumb is such a valuable index to character and temperament.

The characteristics of the thumb, in general, are those of the type of hand to which it belongs, but there are certain special features of the thumb that are worthy of attention. First of all, let us mention the rare case where the thumb is absent or is very small—this is perhaps a sign denoting degeneration to a primitive type. Ordinarily the thumb, when placed close to the index-finger, reaches to the joint or just below it. If it does not reach this joint, it is a short thumb. If it goes beyond the joint the thumb is said to be long.

The thumb has only two phalanges—the first or topmost one is associated with willpower and executive ability, and the second with logical perception and reasoning powers. The size of the first phalange is important in reading the hand, for if the phalange is large it denotes that other tendencies indicated by the fingers and other parts of the hand are likely to be effective. If the contrary is the case, tendencies remain dormant unless there is enough willpower to ensure that these gifts can be actively employed.

The thumb, then, is a real index to character. By the proportionate size of the two phalanges it denotes whether will or reason will have the upper hand in guiding the actions of the subject—if both phalanges are much the same in size, the individual will employ both these mental faculties equally in determining his or her way of life. At the base of the thumb is the mount of Venus, indicating the love propensity. If well developed, it shows that the subject is swayed by his or her heart a good deal in coming to decisions. Palmists sometimes describe the part of the thumb beneath the mount as the third phalange.

If the thumb lies close to the fingers, we can say that the owner is careful with money and not too generous. A looser thumb, standing away from the hand, denotes a freer, more open nature. Then, too, we can note whether the thumb is supple at the top joint, or stiff and unyielding. In the former case we may say the subject is broadminded, generous, tolerant and good-humoured; moreover, he or she can readily adapt to different circumstances. In the person with the stiff-jointed thumb we should expect qualities that are almost the opposite of those just mentioned—caution, reserve, an obstinate adherence to somewhat narrow views of life and morals, and a determination to obtain what are regarded as rights. With this sign should be considered the relative sizes of the first and second phalange.

It is useful to have some standard by which to measure the relative size of the two phalanges of the thumb. Various proportions have been suggested as the normal one. It may be taken that the first or end phalange should be nearly half the length of the thumb, the second being slightly longer. In the left hand it is likely that the phalanges will show quite a different proportional size. When examining a left-handed subject, the left hand should be taken as the representative one.

Sometimes the thumb is broadened and 'clubbed' at

the tip, which is full and plump. This denotes a passionate, hot-tempered individual, swayed excessively by his or her emotions and easily roused to intense anger.

More about the Fingers

The fingers, as you will see, are divided by two knuckles or 'knots' into three divisions.

The top space, which includes the tips with the nails at the back, is the first phalange, devoted to will, as is the top of the thumb. If this is long, fine or pointed, there is also imagination—length indicates the will to express artistic imagination. If thick, an obstinate will. If thick and long, a strong, dominating will. But the thumb ought not to be set low on the hand if the talent is original or creative.

The middle or second phalange belongs to reason. If this is long, then the person thinks things out and, if the hand is fairly square and capable-looking, he or she is able to plan ahead. Good organizers have a strong second phalange. A short space stands for those who have no use for reason. But with a clever hand, intuition will serve the subject well. He or she will 'get there' by trusting his or her own perceptions and acting on first impressions.

The third phalange, if thick and long, belongs to people of a passionate nature. But this phalange of the fingers shows the nobler aspect of the animal nature, just as that at the very base of the hand under Venus, coming as it does in the lowest part of the hand, expresses the physical side.

As for the knots that divide the phalanges, the upper knot dividing the first from the second phalange is the knot of philosophy. Large and well developed, it shows a love of accurate thinking, of exact knowledge. If small, it indicates those who are not at all philosophical, those whose acts are not ruled by their heads. Impetuous people generally have poor knots of philosophy.

The lower knot, which divides the second from the third phalange, is the knot of order. It belongs to great talkers. These are also good talkers, for we generally do well in what we enjoy doing most. People who talk well must have a well-developed sense of order, although they are seldom credited with this. Yet, without it, how could they find the right word and set it in the right place at the right moment?

In a long and narrow hand, a knot that is prominent will show a contradictory, contentious, quarrelsome person. But in a clever, short hand that is wide, indicating kindness, it means a love of debate, a talent for 'stating a case' and ability to prove things. With a crooked little finger, you might get a clever liar, if this knot is strong. But where there is sympathy (a wide hand), and a thumb set low (talent), and good head and heart lines, these talkers generally turn their talent to their own advantage.

The Fingernails

The nails are developed from skin tissues, and so partake of the intimate nature of the flesh. It is remarkable that in people of mixed blood the nails may denote this fact. Even when the blood has been thinned down for a number of generations, the nails may still show signs of ancestry. Then, too, the nails show signs of disease, for example, becoming curved inwards in consumption or tuberculosis. Clubbed fingers are another symptom of this disorder. It is common knowledge that in some cases of poisoning the harmful substance may show its presence when the nails are subjected to chemical examination.

Long nails denote a calm, phlegmatic temperament— short ones suggest a more impetuous nature. When the finger nails are well formed, with good crescents and a rounded, shapely base, we may expect an equable nature and sound judgement. A broad and curved top, associated with the last-named characteristics, denotes an open, generous and frank mind. Narrow, elongated nails are found on people of somewhat delicate constitution, and are often pale and bloodless or even bluish in colour. When unaccompanied by any signs of ill health, the long and moderately narrow nail suggests a refined and idealistic or psychic type of individual. Nails with a spatulate end, especially when broad in proportion to their length, denote pugnacity. When the nails show a reddish colouring, this attribute is strengthened.

In general, the nails should be pinkish to reddish in hue, and not pale or bluish. Ridged or grooved nails suggest a naturally nervous temperament, although this sign may denote nothing more than an alert and sensitive mind. Any irregularities in the shape, form or colouring of the nails are signs of health defects. Blueness that persists is a sign of some defect of the circulatory system. The nails are of secondary importance to the fingers as an index to character, although they may afford useful indications to health and temperament.

The Lines of the Hand

The **line of life** (A) runs around the base of the mount of Venus.

The **line of head** (B) runs across the centre of the hand, starting under Jupiter.

The **line of heart** (C) runs across the upper part of the palm directly under the mounts.

The **line of fate** (D) (or **line of destiny**) is one of the two most important lines on the hand, the other being the line of life. It runs from low down on the hand straight through the centre, up towards the finger of Saturn.

The **line of fortune** (E) (or the **line of Apollo** or the **Sun**) also runs up the hand towards the finger of Apollo, or the ring finger.

The **line of intuition** (F) is rare in its perfect form. It is a semicircle, a longish semicircle or oval line running round or partly round the mount of Luna.

The **girdle of Venus** (G) is rare. When found, it is above the heart line, a small half-circular mark around or partly around the two middle mounts of Jupiter and Saturn.

The **line of Mars** (H) is a smaller half-circle sometimes found within the line of life.

The **line of health** (J) (or the **line of Mercury**), on which business affairs is also read, is a third line running up the hand, but somewhat transversely, towards the finger of Mercury.

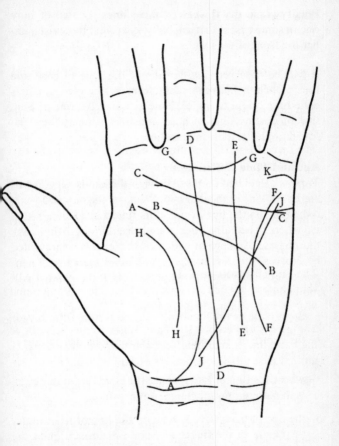

The principal lines of the hand

Finally come the **Bracelets**, three lines (or two or only one in some cases) that run halfway around the wrists, under the front of the hand.

It will be observed that the line of life, line of head and line of health between them form a triangle, which is called the 'great triangle'. Note also that the line of Sun, line of destiny, line of head and line of heart form the 'quadrangle' at their intersection.

Age and Time Calculations

Time is calculated on these lines of the hands, as you will see by looking at the diagram. We have one hundred years to be read on the line of life at its fullest and longest, that is, when it actually goes round and almost behind the thumb base. The age at which certain events, represented by crosses, squares, triangles, and other marks, will happen can be calculated fairly accurately if the palmist will remember:

- the middle of the line of life stands for the fiftieth year

- the centre of the head line represents the age of thirty-five

- where the line of fate touches the head line at its centre is this same important age of thirty-five

- the age of thirty-five is read on the line of heart under the centre of the finger of Apollo. Palmistry gives the larger half of heart events to the years before thirty-five.

In real life, as in palmistry, we 'count time by heartbeats' and not by hours or years. It is a mistake to think that all hours—or years—are exactly the same length.

Doubtless the most interesting marks to be found among the minor lines of the hand, which indicate voyages, change of environment, talents and ambitions, are those that concern the attachments, love affairs and future marriage of the subject.

These are the influence lines, which may be discerned running from the mount of Luna to the line of fate, from the mount of Venus to the line of life, and on the mount of Mercury. Their depth, length and clarity depend upon the enduring nature of the sentiment involved. When crossed, barred or cut, they demonstrate the fact that difficulties and opposition from parents, friends or relatives are to be encountered, or it may be that the influence was merely a fleeting infatuation.

These signs should be compared with the age calculated upon the fate line—it will then be discovered whether the influence lines are of the past, present or future. Only constant practice and experience can aid the reader to a correct estimate of the period of these happenings.

How to Read the Lines
Date Lines
The chronology used in palmistry is based upon a division of certain of the lines into year-periods. The line of heart, line of head, line of destiny, line of Sun and line of life are those chiefly used for determining ages or dates. The span

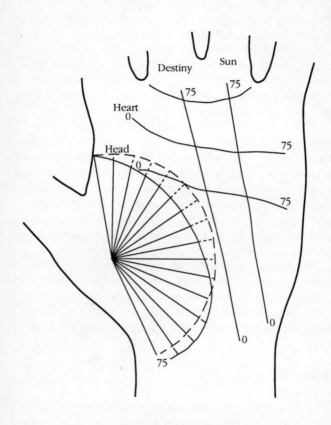

Date lines

of a human being's life can be taken at 75 years for the purpose of these readings, and the lines are graduated accordingly. The line of life reads downwards, and the lines of destiny and the Sun are read upwards. The lines of heart and head are read from their origin at the thumb side of the palm.

These lines can be divided into four-, six- or seven-year intervals, or, as in this text, a five-year interval.

The Line of Life
The line of life, long, even and clear, represents a long and healthy life. If broken in one hand, this life line tells of a serious illness. If completely broken in both hands, then life may end at that age. However, the life line may grow again and the broken lines join together, especially if more than five years lie between the date at which the hand is read and the time when the life lines in both hands end. Thus, no serious palmist would pretend to be able to tell the age at which death occurs.

Note that this life line, if chained, tells of delicacy and illness, caused by anxiety, unhappiness or worry. If the line is red, there is a tendency to fevers. If it is purple, it shows a tendency to inherited illnesses. One often sees a faint purplish shade on part of the line of life of one hand. If in the left hand only, this shows actual illness has been avoided.

Both hands must be read, and when the life line shows a series of fine crosses set closely together, this indicates the occurrence of neuralgic pains and aches at the time indicated. If these are repeated on the line of head, then this indicates pain of a more serious nature, occurring in the head. This life line, pale or thin, tells of general poor health during those years. But the smaller line of Mars inside the life line promises survival, and corrects or modifies indications of poor health or of short life.

Branches upwards from the line of life tell of honours or successes that are purely fortuitous. Thus, if an individual achieves high office, his or her palm will show a branch upwards from the line of fate. This individual's partner, for whom this honour is fortuitous, might show a branch on the life line.

The Line of Head

When this line is long there is talent and a naturally good memory. But if it is too closely linked up with the beginning of the line of life (thus making only one line under the mount of Jupiter) there is a marked lack of self-confidence. If they continue as one for over 12 mm (half an inch), then this self-distrust will greatly hamper and delay success, however talented the subject is.

The line of head starting slightly apart from the life line gives a steady self-confidence. But if the space between is very wide (7 mm—1/5th of an inch—is very wide here), this shows rash impulsiveness. Review and re-evaluation will always be advisable for these people.

The head line, if short, shows impulse, prejudice, a lack of reasoning power and a tendency to act first and think afterwards. The line of head when straight and long shows thrift and economy (with no imagination, if very straight). Long and tending slightly downwards at the end shows sympathy and an ability to see the viewpoint of other people. If drooping low down to the base of the hand, the subject has too much imagination. If apparent in both hands, along with a weak thumb, then it may indicate mental weakness.

If the line of head is divided into a large fork at the end, one branch of which goes straight across the hand and the other turns down on to the mount of Luna or even towards the wrist, this shows that life has two sides—the practical side, which will be efficiently conducted, and a vivid and very real life of the imagination. The hands of novelists typically show this handsome forking on the head lines.

If the head line is blurred, this indicates an illness in which there has been delirium. If it is broken in one hand, the subject may commit a serious error of judgement. A line broken in both hands is a warning that the subject may suffer an accident where his or her head is injured in some way.

The Line of Heart

When this is clear and long, it gives a happy life, rich in affection. But if it misses the mount of Jupiter, rising from up between that mount and the next one, the mount of Saturn, there is coldness as regards love, with a tormenting capacity for jealousy. If this is apparent on one hand only, this tendency is kept under control admirably. Hands in which the heart line misses Jupiter do not find happiness in love. When it starts under Saturn there is coldness and a lack of feeling.

A short heart line denotes selfishness in love, where

flirting takes the place of affection and may be mistaken for it. A series of very small crosses on the heart line indicates suffering through the unworthiness of those loved.

A broken heart line shows a broken engagement or similar emotional trauma. Breaks under the mount of Jupiter indicate the cause was honour; under Saturn, this indicates that the cause was a fatality, perhaps death; under Apollo, pride with some mystery. The subject does not know *why* the break came and is too proud to find out. Under Mercury, the broken heart line means that the person who was loved was thoroughly unworthy.

The Girdle of Venus

The girdle of Venus used to be read as a sign of an evil life. Now, however, it is more correctly taken to mean the likelihood of some great unhappiness regarding an emotional attachment. Its ugly aspect will have passed over by the time the subject reaches his or her thirty-fifth year.

If a man has this half-ring, he will be well advised not to marry until that age has passed, nor indeed to form any important partnerships. If a married woman is seen to have this girdle, the wise palmist will tell her to 'sit tight'. She will surely get on better with her unsatisfactory life partner *after* she has turned thirty-five. This ill-omened mark also tells of sudden death touching the life. The girdle of Venus always tells of a catastrophe that has occurred in the earlier part of the life

The Line of Fate

This may start from four places:

• From the bracelets—this indicates an uncommon destiny that may mean great happiness or misery, according to the way in which the life is lived. However, the circumstances are, as a rule, out of the subject's choice with this 'start' of the fate line.

- From the line of life—this shows a good life with good chances. The subject makes his or her own way in life.

- From the mount of Luna—fate is made by marriage or entirely through the decisions or doings of other people.

- From the middle of the hand—a hard life, troubled and hampered by poverty or cruel circumstances.

But the line of fate that ends high up in the hand, even though it starts over high up, *does* spell success at the end. Breaks in this line are not negative, they represent changes. If the line goes on straight and clear, these may be good changes. Branches towards the Moon tell of travels. Branches towards Jupiter tell of honours and dignities earned.

Branches that rise from the outer side and touch the fate line denote affairs of the heart. Those that are clear and touch the fate lines of both hands indicate marriage at the age where they touch. A good cross on Jupiter ought to confirm this indication.

Sometimes the fate line, after starting well and low down in the hand, disappears for some years and then reappears. This means that the life is uneventful during those years. The money line also disappears sometimes. Widowhood, represented by a line from the fate line touching the heart line and ending in a cross, often brings out both the fate line and the money line again, later on in life. This is only if the widow obtains control of money because of her bereavement.

Absence of the fate line does not mean anxiety. It shows that the person is only 'vegetating' when there is no fate line. Small lines across the fate line are troubles.

The Line of Fortune

This tells of money matters. When it drops for some time it has the same meaning as the fading of the fate line. This line, chained or blurred, tells of actual struggling, of 'hard times' due to the absence of money or to expenditure being more than income.

A long clear line going right up to the mount of Apollo tells of riches, a successful life as regards financial fortune. If it bites into the finger, then there is a kind of 'glorious' fortune, great inheritance or a fortune received through some kind of 'luck'.

The Line of Business and of Health

This shows the career, if indeed there is one. This line, standing out prominently and going straight up to the mount of Mercury, speaks of a successful career. Branches jutting out signify tests, adventures and experiences in new lines of work. If these last while the original line fades out, then this indicates that there will be a clear change of occupation. If forked at the top, this line shows there is great practical ability in the individual. If it is thick, this indicates a delicate old age; if it is red and thin, this shows feverish tendencies. Beware of excitement if this line looks 'angry'.

The Line of Intuition

The line of intuition gives great sympathy, instinctive cleverness, intuitive judgment. Perfectly formed, this line belongs to the 'seer', the clairvoyant. Being on the mount of the Moon, it implies sadness, even unhappiness:

'For foresight is a melancholy gift
Which bares the bald and speeds the all-too swift.'

The Bracelets

These tell of successful life, money, and gains in general. It is said that each of these lines, if it is clear and deep (but not too wide) indicates some thirty years of joyful living. But if one of the lines or some part of any of them is chained, there is a fight against poverty and difficult circumstances during that period of thirty years, or the part of them that is chained.

The bracelets are read as beginning from the end under the thumb. The one nearest the hand stands for the first 30 years of life; the centre line for the period between 30 and 60 years. These are years of effort and struggle in any life that is lived in an honourable way. The lowest line represents the period between 60 and 90 years. You can understand why few hands have these three lines clear and unbroken!

Branches on any age of the lines tell of legacies. The year, in which the legacy or the various legacies are re-

ceived can be accurately computed by means of the age
instructions already given.

The Triangle

Note that the lines of head, life and fate should form a
well-defined triangle under the two middle fingers. If this
triangle is weak at the junction of any two of the three
lines, look for failure or disappointment affecting the destiny of the subject in connection with the qualities represented by those two lines.

Thus, if the triangle is cramped owing to the head line
being joined to the life line, then a lack of self-confidence
hinders success. If the head line spoils the triangle, owing
to its going far down on the mount of Luna instead of
straight across the middle of the hand, a too active imagination is the enemy. With warm affections, a too imagina-
tive head line spells jealousy.

If the life line stops short and so spoils the triangle, life
is cut short and success hindered by this. The fate line
weak or poor or absent in the early part of life sometimes
spoils the shape of the triangle. In this case, early hard-
ships, struggles, lack of friends, etc, may cause failure.

The Plain of Mars

The plain of Mars is the space between the two mounts of
that name. It lies between the lines of the heart and of the
head, and should be clear and wide. That is, the heart line
should not drop into it nor the head line rise up on to it. If
it is hollow, then this plain is said to show early exile from
home. If this plain is clear and well defined in the left

hand, it indicates skill in chess and in strategy—in the
right hand, with other indications of courage, bravery
with skill.

Reading Both Hands

Note that the left hand stands for the natural and the *fated*
things, the right hand for what we do with them. The right
hand is the hand of *free will*. If one hand is distinctly
'bad', showing a poor fate line, crossed and broken, or a
badly broken line of fortune, it is better for this to be the
left hand, because the right hand *may* show improvement.
In this case, there will have been a brave fight and the
fighter has made things better than they were originally.

If the left hand is 'good' and the right one 'bad', then
this says that good health has been wasted, money prospects lost sight of, and hopeful chances thrown away. It is
important never to 'tell' anything really important until
you have found it to be so in both hands.

Now let us study the small signs and symbols on the lines
and the mounts:

Crosses

Crosses are bad when they are badly formed. A well-
formed cross on Jupiter's mount stands for a good marriage. On Saturn's mount, ill-luck. When Saturn's line
(the line of fate) goes up into the actual finger, ending
there with a cross, there is a great and uncommon destiny,
with tragedy at the ending.

A cross on the line of fate is always an obstacle, a
'check' to the fate.

A cross lying near it, but not on it, is an obstacle to a life near. Note that the line of fate that stops short in the middle of the hand indicates failure, however well it starts up.

A cross on Apollo's mount means ill-luck connected with art or literature. On the mount of Mercury, it shows a loss of money or ill-gotten gains. On the line of intuition it shows delusions, on the line of life, it indicates an illness. A cross beside the line of life points to illness or trouble to some life near. A cross in the plain of Mars (in the middle of the palm under Saturn) signifies love of the Occult, attraction to magic, etc.

Stars

Stars are fatalities. One on the mount of Jupiter indicates honours. On the mount of Saturn, you find the signs of danger of death by violence. On the mount of Apollo, it indicates unhappy riches. On the mount of Mercury, theft or dishonour may be indicated. A star in the plain of Mars, that is, between the two mounts of Mars, signifies military glory. On the mount of Luna, a star may be indicative of danger of drowning. A star low on the head line points to insanity in the family—high up on the head line it is a signal of danger of loss of sight. A star on line of fortune signifies catastrophe.

Squares

Squares are good. They add force and strength to the qualities indicated by the mounts where they appear. But a square on the inside of the line of life represents imprison-

ment or seclusion of some kind. Note the age at which the
square touches the life line.

Triangles

Triangles indicate some special talent or aptitude—on Jupiter for diplomacy, on Saturn for magic, on Apollo for art
or literature, on Mercury for success (money success) in
politics. A triangle on the mount of Venus tells of a prudent marriage. Triangles also represent deliverance from
danger and misfortune.

Dots

Dots are sometimes of good *or* evil omen. White dots on
the heart line tell of success in love. Red dots on the heart
line point to emotional love affairs. Dark dots on the head
line indicate eye trouble. White dots on the head line success in invention, according to which mount they appear
under.

Islands

Islands that are made by the line dividing and then joining
up again about 12 mm (half an inch) further on are always
bad. On the life line they tell of hereditary illness. On the
heart line, an unworthy attachment is indicated. On the
health line they tell of the same illness as on the life line,
but this, though serious, is not fatal.

Grills

Grills or crossed lines always show obstacles. They take
from the good effects of the qualities indicated by the

mounts, just as squares add to these qualities. A grill on Jupiter tells of tyranny and superstition. On Saturn it denotes misfortune. On Apollo a grill indicates folly, vanity and extravagance. On Mercury it is a sign of hypocrisy, lying and theft. A grill on Mars tells of sudden death and on Luna it signifies anxiety, discontent, sadness.

Marriage

Marriage is indicated by a large cross on the mount of Jupiter. Again, the marriage line comes up from the outer side of the hand under the mount of the little finger and crosses Mercury. The branches that rise on either side of this clear line are indicative of children. If it drops on to the line of heart, widowhood is likely. If it crosses the heart line to the plain of Mars, this tells of a possible separation, also to be read in the lines of influence that rise on Luna's mount and go up to the fate line. When these touch in both hands, there is a strong likelihood of marriage taking place at that age. But it is the experience of all palmists that an attachment will show as clearly, sometimes more clearly, in the hand of a single person than actual marriage in the hands of frivolous people. Even the cross is occasionally found on the mount of Jupiter in the hands of lifelong celibates, but it is blurred or marred in some way.

Postscript

While the ancient subject of palmistry amply repays more profound study by those who wish to devote themselves to it, it is possible to read any hand thoroughly, to tell the character, the weak points, and the actual events from the beginning to the end of life, from a knowledge of the principles and practice as described.

Whether it be palmistry, however, or any of the other methods of forecasting events, telling fortunes or reading character, the chief point to strike us is the age of all these methods. With practically no modification they have been handed down to us through the ages. They do not change with the march of time and their very antiquity should bring them veneration and respect.

Many of the superstitions in particular are not confined to our own land but prevail in other countries and it is a fact that in the Middle Ages palmistry, or *cheiromancy* as it was then called, was numbered among the forbidden black arts.

Superstitions

What is a Superstition?

At some time in our lives, all of us will have been guided in our actions by superstition. Whether we have avoided walking under a ladder, or taken a lucky pen to use in an examination, whether we have thrown spilt salt over our shoulder or never worn a certain colour, it all comes down to the same thing: a belief, or a wish to believe, or even a fear of not believing, that our future can be influenced by events and things that probably have no obvious bearing upon it.

Belief in superstitions also gives us the idea that we can, to some degree at least, see what lies ahead of us in the future. Good or bad, people have always wanted to have some idea of their destinies, or of those aspects of their lives over which they feel they have no control. Superstitious beliefs can also give people the impression that they can have some degree of control over their destinies, whether by avoiding certain courses of action or, conversely, by performing certain rituals.

If we were to think more logically about superstitious behaviour, our thoughts would be more like the following—'A rabbit's foot is sometimes used as a good luck charm. Will carrying a rabbit's foot around in my pocket help me to pass my driving test? Probably not. A thorough knowledge of the Highway Code is helpful, but a rabbit's foot has nothing to do with my knowledge of the highway code, nor with my ability to manoeuvre round a corner in reverse.'

Indeed, if you were to stop and think of all the little rabbits that have been squashed on the road in the years since the invention of the motor car, you might well come to the conclusion that a rabbit's foot, of all things, is perhaps the least likely to bring good luck in a driving test. Why would a rabbit's foot bless the progress of another killer onto the roads?

Some superstitious behaviour does have a degree of logic about it. For example, the superstition that it is unlucky to walk under a ladder probably has its origins in religious beliefs. But it does also have a certain amount of common sense behind it. Walking underneath a ladder, especially if someone is working at the top of it, is not always the safest path to take.

Superstitions can be very convenient. We can choose whether or not to believe in them given the circumstances of the moment, knowing, if we choose not to believe, that we have the safety net of saying that it is all a lot of superstitious nonsense. Thus, if our experiments to find out the name of our true love, for example, do not come up with a pleasing result, we can happily ignore them, i.e. choose not to believe in them. If they come up with the result that we desire, we can then pronounce that we knew it to be true all along.

For every superstition that bodes ill, there is another that foretells of good fortune, so, to a certain extent, we

can pick and choose from the folklore with which we are
familiar, in order to select the future that we would prefer
to think of ourselves as having.

To believe in every superstition with which you have
become acquainted would undoubtedly cause much confusion. What, for example, about the occurrence of omi-
nous happenings in sequence? What if you were to see a
black cat cross your path and then see a solitary magpie?
Does this mean that the bad luck of seeing a solitary magpie cancels out the good luck of having a black cat cross
your path? Or is one occurrence a stronger influence on
future events than the other, and, if so, which? Or are you
destined to have a spell of good luck swiftly followed by a
spell of bad luck? Who is to say?

The tie between superstition and religious beliefs cannot be ignored either. Some superstitions have their foundation in religious stories or beliefs.

Religious icons may be kept as a symbol of a person's
beliefs, but in many cases they are kept more as good luck
charms. St Christopher medallions, for example, are often
worn by people irrespective of whether they have religious convictions.

Superstitions can be personal, as in the case of the
'lucky' exam pen, or they can be common to whole com-
munities, or even have influences worldwide. Superstitions may be as old as the hills, or they may be the result
of a more contemporary folklore. Superstitious behaviour,
in all its manifestations, can be found worldwide, and
while the origins of some superstitions may be unclear to
say the least, they are certainly fascinating to study. Listed

alphabetically below are many of the beings and objects that have superstitions connected with them.

A

acorn an acorn carried in the pocket will act as a guarantee of youthfulness and longevity.

animals there are many superstitions associated with animals.

bat: many believe that a bat flying close to you is unlucky, especially if you hear it squeak as it approaches. Nevertheless, bats are not despised by all superstitions, for many people believe that is lucky to have bats nesting in your house. Nowadays, as bats become rarer, especially in urban settings, it should certainly be seen as a privilege.

cat: the cat is associated with a great many superstitions. Watch your cat carefully—cats are supposed to have a certain amount of extrasensory perception. Strange behaviour in your cat may be its reaction to something that it has sensed that is beyond your perception. Does the cat appear nervous or frightened in your new house? There may be ghosts!

If your cat sneezes three times, count the sneezes. One sneeze is considered to be lucky, but three sneezes and you should prepare for an outbreak of colds and coughs in the family.

If a cat suddenly and unaccountably leaves home, some bad fortune will befall the family.

If you kill a cat, or even just tread on its tail, you will be very unlucky.

A black cat crossing your path will bring you good luck, but a white one is unlucky.

If a stray black cat should venture into your home, you should make it welcome, for this will bring you great good fortune.

Cats are also supposed to be able to forecast the weather. If your cat sits with its back to the fire, a storm is likely. If it spends too long washing itself, prepare for wet weather. If it seems to be inordinately frisky, the wind could soon become a gale.

dog: dogs, like cats, are believed to have extrasensory perception and are supposed to have the ability to sense death and to see ghosts. Thus, a dog who howls without reason at the door is often seen as an omen of imminent death in the household.

Many people believe that dogs have a sense of 'good' and 'bad' people and that a person whom your dog takes a dislike to for no apparent reason may be an undesirable person to have as a friend. It is also widely believed that if you are followed home by a stray dog, this is a sign of good luck.

hare: a hare crossing your path is widely held to be an omen of ill-fortune, and a hare passing a house foretells a fire in the house in the future. At one time it was believed that witches chose to disguise themselves as hares.

hedgehog: hedgehogs are generally thought to be lucky creatures. Passing a hedgehog on the road is a sign of good luck to come. Of course, killing a hedgehog is consequently unlucky.

horse: a white horse may be lucky; if you see one you should make a wish. If you meet a white horse whilst out with your beloved, it is said that you can be sure of happiness together in the future.

A piebald horse is also believed to be lucky, but only if you meet it head-on.

Finding a horseshoe is widely believed to bring good luck, but you must keep it after you find it if you want the luck to stay with you.

lamb: the lamb is the sign of peace and love in superstition as much as in religion. Meeting a lamb out on its own is a sign of good luck.

mouse: a gift of a white mouse will be lucky for you, but a grey mouse will not bring good fortune.

mule: mules are thought to be unlucky, and a sign of treachery.

rabbit: rabbits have come to be regarded by some as symbols of fertility and fruitfulness; this idea most likely has its origins in the prolific breeding habits of the rabbit.

The belief that a rabbit's foot will bring luck and offer protection from harm is one that is held in many places throughout the world; to carry a rabbit's foot is lucky and, conversely, to lose one is most unfortunate.

On the first day of every month, many people consider that it is important to say 'white rabbits' three times for luck.

toad: to find a toad sitting in one's path is thought to be a sign of money to come. Killing a toad is said to bring rain.

ant *see* INSECTS.

apple the apple is principally associated with superstitions concerning affairs of the heart, probably because of its associations with Adam and Eve. If a girl is able to peel an apple in one piece without breaking the peel, she should throw it over her left shoulder. If, on examining the peel after it has fallen, she is able to make out the shape of a letter, this is thought to be the first initial of the man whom she will marry. If the peel breaks into more than one piece when it falls to the floor, then the girl will not marry.

If you are uncertain as to whether your feelings of affection for another are likely to be returned, eat an apple and then throw a seed on the fire, saying as you do so, the name of the one you love. If the apple seed makes a popping sound as it burns, then you can rest easy that your love is not unrequited!

It is thought to be lucky if you do not pick up all the windfalls from your apple tree, but instead leave one or two where they lie on the ground.

Many people in Great Britain hold the belief that to see apple blossom and fruit on the same tree at the same time is a bad omen that means that there will be a death in the family.

apron it is thought to be unlucky to put an apron on inside out; if you do so, you should prepare yourself for an accident-prone day.

If you wear an apron, tie it on firmly as it is thought to be unlucky if your apron falls off while you are wearing it.

ashes ashes have come to be associated in many places
throughout the world with fertility. In some countries,
they were believed to encourage healthy growth and
were mixed in with animal feed. Ashes scattered over
crops or mixed in with seeds prior to sowing were believed to encourage a healthy crop.

aspen *see* TREES.

B

babies there are countless superstitions concerning babies
worldwide, probably stemming from the anxiety all
mothers feel about their babies and the responsibilities
of bringing up a child.

> *Monday's child is fair of face*
> *Tuesday's child is full of grace*
> *Wednesday's child is full of woe*
> *Thursday's child has far to go*
> *Friday's child is loving and giving*
> *Saturday's child works hard for a living*
> *But the child that is born on the Sabbath day*
> *Is bonny and bright and good and gay.*

It is said that a baby who is born with a caul over his or
her face will be lucky and grow to be rich.

A child who is born at twilight, when the light is poor,
will grow up with second sight.

A baby who is born on Good Friday will grow used to
sadness throughout its life but will, however, have the
gift of easing other people through their own pain and
distress.

A child who is born on All Hallows Eve (Hallowe'en) will be blessed with the gift of second sight.

A newly born baby is said to be in danger from the fairies until it first sneezes. From that moment on, it will be able to stay safely in the human world.

Rocking an empty cradle has two different superstitions attached to it—one is that a woman who rocks an empty cradle will have many babies, the other is that to rock an empty cradle means that the baby who usually sleeps in the cradle will die young.

If a baby's first tooth appears in its lower jaw, this is said to mean that the child will live long. If the baby grows teeth early, it is said that another child will be born in the family within a short time.

Many people believe that a baby should not see its own reflection in a mirror until six months after its birth, for a child who sees itself in a mirror before the age of six months will die before it is a year old.

It is believed to be better for a mother to nibble off the nails of her young baby with her teeth, because to cut a baby's nails before it is twelve months old is said to mean that the child will grow up to be light-fingered.

Dressing a baby in black is thought to be unlucky and to foretell an early death for the child.

If a baby laughs or crows and kicks with its little hands open, it is said that the child will grow up open-handed and generous. A child who keeps its fingers firmly curled together, however, will grow up to be close-fisted, or mean. *See also* CHRISTENINGS.

bat *see* ANIMALS.

bed place the head of your bed towards the south and you
will live long; place it towards the north and you will
have a short life. If the head of your bed is placed towards the west, you will travel far—to the east, you will
be wealthy.

It is believed to be unlucky to turn a mattress on a bed
on a Friday or a Sunday—such folly puts you at risk of
bad dreams until the mattress is turned again.

bees *see* INSECTS.

beetles *see* INSECTS.

bellows in the days when bellows were used to blow life
into the fire, it was considered unlucky to place the bellows on the table or to leave them lying on the floor as
leaving them in either place meant quarrels would follow within the household.

birds many superstitions concern birds. It is considered
unlucky for a bird to fly in to a house through an open
window. A swallow entering a house through a chimney
foretells a death in the household.

It is also considered to be unlucky to keep an injured
wild bird in the house.

cockerel: If a cock crows with its head facing towards
the house, there will be a visit from a stranger shortly.

If a girl is thinking of her sweetheart and hears the
sound of a cockerel crowing, it is thought to be lucky,
but if a man or woman hears a cockerel crowing on his or
her wedding day, the marriage may not be harmonious.

An encounter with a white cockerel is thought to be
unlucky.

crow: it is considered to be unlucky to see a crow standing on one leg, to have a crow flying and cawing round about your house, or to see two crows fighting outside your house.

If you hear the sound of a crow cawing, try the following to see what the future has in store—placing one foot right in front of the other, pace out the length of your shadow in footsteps. Add thirteen to this number, then divide the result by six. If the remainder is one, then you will be lucky, but two can only mean trouble and sorrow in store. Three means great happiness to come, four means you will never want for food and five means that you will be blessed with riches in later life.

cuckoo: to hear the first cuckoo of spring too early, in March, may bring you ill-fortune. If you hear it whilst lying in bed, you can expect to suffer from ill-health.

If you see a cuckoo and it is standing still, you are likely to remain settled where you are for some time, but to see a cuckoo take off into flight presages a move of some sort, or travel for the person who sees it.

For those who seek to know when they will marry, the sound of the cuckoo can help. On hearing the first cuckoo of the year, they should kiss their hand and wave it towards the sound of the cuckoo's call, saying as they do—'Cuckoo, tell me true, when shall I be married?'

When they hear the cuckoo again, they should count the number of its calls before it becomes silent once more. The number of calls will be the number of years that will pass before the wedding takes place.

To hear a cuckoo on the right hand side means that

prosperity will come, but to hear it on the left is a sign of bad luck ahead.

dove: the dove is a sign of love and happiness and it is especially lucky for lovers who set eyes on it together.

duck: the sound of a quacking duck is thought by some to be lucky, as is the sight of a duck in flight.

eagle: the sound of the cry of an eagle in flight is thought to be a warning of doom.

geese: geese make very useful 'watchbirds', and possibly as a consequence of this, the sound of cackling geese is thought to be a warning of dangers unseen.

hen: if you hear a hen crowing like a cockerel instead of clucking as it should, bad luck, or more particularly, poor health may follow.

magpie: it is believed by some that to see a magpie flying from right to left across your path will bring you bad luck.

More generally, it is believed to be unlucky to see a solitary magpie. This idea perhaps has its origins in the fact that it is more common to see magpies in pairs. To see one on its own, therefore, suggests that somehow all is not right.

It is said by some people that one way of fending off the bad luck of seeing a single magpie is to look at the bird and speak to it, saying, 'Good morning, Mr. Magpie.' Alternatively, you could try spitting three times over your left shoulder.

If you see one magpie, always look around for others; there probably will be at least one other. Count them and remember this rhyme:

> *One's sorrow, two's mirth,*
> *Three's a wedding, four's a birth,*
> *Five's a christening, six a death,*
> *Seven's heaven, eight is hell,*
> *And nine is the devil his ane sel'.*

owl: owls are generally considered to be quite unlucky. It is thought to be unlucky to hear an owl hooting at night and to hear it hooting three times in succession bodes particularly ill as it may foretell that you will hear of someone's death.

peacock: peacock's feathers should not be brought into the house as this is considered to be very unlucky indeed. The 'eye' in a male peacock's tail feathers is thought to be evil.

It is considered to be lucky to see a peacock spreading out its feathers in courtship display.

raven: the raven, much like the crow, is generally considered to be a bird of ill-fortune. It is thought to be an omen of death to hear a raven crowing over your house.

The ravens that inhabit the Tower of London are famous worldwide, as is the superstition associated with them that if for some reason they all die, or fly away, or simply disappear, disaster will fall upon the country and its royal family.

robin: it is said that whoever hurts a robin or a wren will never prosper on land or at sea.

birthplace it is considered to be lucky to visit the place of your birth when you have grown up, as it is believed to bring you long life.

black *see* COLOUR.

blackberry *see* TREES AND BUSHES.

bones burning beef bones is thought to be unlucky and to bring poverty and sorrow. Burning chicken bones means that you will be the subject of malicious gossip.

bottle look after glass bottles carefully, as it is unlucky to break them.

bracken *see* PLANTS.

bread the idea of the baker's dozen, i.e. thirteen, is thought to come from an old belief that the baker had to keep his peace with the Devil and thus baked 'twelve for the baker and one for the Devil.'

If you are slicing bread and the slices are uneven, you may have been telling lies. If the bread crumbles as you slice it, beware of family quarrels.

Wasting bread is unlucky—if you throw it away today, you will go hungry later.

brown *see* COLOUR.

bush if you snag your clothes on a bush by accident whilst out walking, you may be about to come into some money.

button fasten your buttons carefully, for it is believed to be bad luck to fasten them up wrongly and put them into the wrong buttonholes.

C

candle candles should always be placed as securely as possible in their holders, for it is said to be unlucky if a candle falls over. This superstition may well have some foundation in the fact that an upset candle is a fire hazard and therefore can indeed bring very bad fortune. And don't forget to make a wish when you blow out the birthday candles! *See also* DEATH.

cat *see* ANIMALS.

chairs a visitor who returns his or her chair back to the place where it came from is unlikely to visit again. Similarly, it is also said that someone who dines at a house for the first time should not push their chair back into the table when they rise, or they will not return to dine at the house again. *See also* CUSHIONS.

chicory *see* PLANTS.

christenings there are many people who still believe that a baby will not thrive properly until it has been christened.

It is considered very lucky for a child to be christened on the same day of the week as that on which it was born.

A baby who cries at his or her own christening is fortunate. The cries are a sign that it is strong enough to fight the influence of evil. A baby that does not cry at its christening is not so lucky, however.

It is believed that the woman who carries the baby to church to be christened should carry a piece of bread and some cheese with her. This should be given to the first person whom she meets, on behalf of the child. If the food is not eaten or if the gift is refused, it is thought to be unlucky. Good fortune will come to the baby if the gift is well-received, particularly if the recipient is poor or needy and eats the bread and cheese immediately.

Christmas 'Christmas lights candles of kindness in the

darkness of winter', it is said, and so it is that most superstitions attached to Christmas time are happy ones.

If a man is lucky enough to kiss a girl under the mistletoe, he should remove one berry for every kiss he is allowed. Optimistic men should therefore hang mistletoe with a good supply of berries!

If a girl has not been kissed under the mistletoe over the Yuletide, she can expect to remain single, for at least a year and a day thereafter.

If you kiss someone under the mistletoe, you will remain on good terms with them always and never quarrel.

If you would like to guarantee weeks and weeks of happiness in the year to come, eat as many mince pies in as many houses as you can over Christmas time. Each mince pie eaten will bring a week of happiness in the coming year.

In the days when it was customary to have a Yuletide log to burn at Christmas, it was thought to be lucky if a small piece of it was not burned and was saved for the following Christmas. Another superstition held that it was unlucky for the Yuletide log to be touched by a woman with a flat foot or a man with a squint!

It is not a good idea to get married on Holy Innocents' Day, nor is it advisable to cut your nails or to wear new clothes for the first time.

On Christmas Eve, a girl who wishes to know who her future true love will be should put her shoes one across the other in the form of the letter 'T' as she goes to bed at night. She should then recite this rhyme:

> *I hope tonight my true love to see—*
> *So I put my shoes in the form of a 'T'.*

Alternatively, the girl could try walking backwards to a pear tree, if there is one nearby, and then circle around it nine times. A vision of her true love may then appear to her.

Good luck will come to those who have a stir of the Christmas pudding. Make a wish as you stir, but do not tell anyone what you have wished for or your wish will not come true.

Whatever you believe in at Christmas, remember that Father Christmas will come !

cigarettes many people, especially older people who remember relatives who fought in the war, believe that it is unlucky to light more than two cigarettes with one match. This is because those who fought in the wars thought that the first light gave snipers first sight of their target, and the second allowed them to take aim. Lighting a third person's cigarette would give a sniper time to shoot at the flaming target that the match provided.

clothes dress carefully! Try not to put on any item of clothing inside out or to fasten any buttons wrongly; you will only be inviting misfortune, or so it is said. If you do put on any clothes inside out, you should keep them on that way for the rest of the day.

Always put some money in the right hand pocket of any coat or jacket that you wear for the first time, or any coat or jacket that you give to someone as a gift. This is said to protect the wearer against pennilessness in the future. A coat worn for the first time without money in the pocket may bring hard times upon the wearer.

If your shoelace comes undone accidentally, without being caught on anything and pulled out, you should be assured that your true love is thinking of you at that very moment.

Gloves are an unlucky gift to give unless the giver receives something in return. *See also* GLOVES.

clover *see* FLOWERS.

coal it is thought to be lucky if you pick up a piece of coal that has fallen in your path. Success is on the way.

If the first person over the threshold on New Year's day is a dark man carrying a piece of coal, you will have good luck that year. *See also* NEW YEAR.

cockerel *see* BIRDS.

colour many people, particularly those in the acting professions, avoid wearing the colour green as it is thought to be unlucky. Some people believe that the wearer of a green dress will soon be wearing the black of mourning. Green is not thought to be unlucky, however, for those people who have birthdays in May.

It is unlucky for anyone—bride, groom or guest—to wear brown to a wedding. Brown is a symbol of gradually fading affection.

It is said that someone who wears brown all year long will be working hard all year for the benefit of somebody else and not for his or her own good.

Although it is the colour of mourning, black is not considered to be an unlucky colour in itself, and is in fact considered to be a good colour for those who have December or August birthdays. It is also considered to be quite lucky to wear a hat that has a touch of black on it. *See also* BABIES.

Orange-red or flame colours worn at a wedding say that the partnership is based on selfishness and fortune-seeking rather than true love.

cooking if you want the food that you are preparing to taste good, you should always stir it in a clockwise direction.

corns if you have corns, wait until the moon is on the wane before you cut them as tradition dictates that this is the best time.

crow *see* BIRDS.

cuckoo *see* BIRDS.

cushions do not plump up the cushion in the chair you have been sitting in if you have been paying someone a visit. As with the replacing of chairs, it is a sign that you are unlikely to visit the house again. *See also* CHAIRS.

D

daisy *see* FLOWERS.

dandelion *see* FLOWERS.

death fears about death, and uncertainty about what happens to us after we die, have spawned a great many superstitious beliefs over the centuries. Many of the superstitions that are included in this book concern omens of death or factors that are believed either to bring about an early death or to prolong life and postpone the end.

Black is the traditional colour to wear at funerals, and

this tradition probably stems from a belief that the mourners should make themselves invisible to evil spirits or the Devil, who may be on the lookout for new souls for his kingdom.

Lighting candles around a coffin has its origins in the belief that the candlelight will ward off evil.

The tolling of bells after a death is believed to drive away evil spirits.

Some believe that those who have died should not be left alone or else they may be claimed by the Devil.

In times past there was often great reluctance shown towards having a family corpse buried in a new cemetery. It was believed that the first dead body in a cemetery would be claimed as a 'tithe'—a kind of supernatural tax—by the Devil.

There is a belief that it is unlucky to see a grave digger coming towards you as this is an indication of serious illness to come.

The opening of doors and windows after a death is often thought to facilitate the passage of the soul to heaven. *See also* GRAVE.

dog *see* ANIMALS.

door it is believed that it is unlucky if the front door of a house does not face the street.

When closing a front door, you should always face it.

Many people believe in the practice of opening a door when there is a birth or a death in the family to make the transition in or out of the world easier. *See also* DEATH.

dove *see* BIRDS.

dreams it is said by some that to have the same dream

three times in a row will mean that the dream is certain to come true.

drink see food and drink.

duck *see* BIRDS.

E

eagle *see* BIRDS.

ears many things are said about the size and shape of people's ears and the personalities that are associated with them. Big ears are generally thought to indicate a generous nature, while small ears point to a certain meanness. Ears that lie very close to the head are said to indicate timidity, even cowardliness, but sticking-out ears are the sign of a fighter.

To feel a tingling sensation in the ears is an indication that someone is talking about you. If your right ear tingles, bad things are being said. If the left ear tingles, someone is speaking favourably about you. As the saying goes—'The left for love and the right for spite.'

eggs burning eggshells should be avoided. There is a belief that if eggshells are burnt, the hen that laid the eggs will stop laying.

It is said that eggs that are laid on Good Friday will stay perfectly fresh for one year.

After eating a boiled egg, crush the shell with your spoon to guard against misfortune. Superstition has it that witches use eggshells as boats.

If you drop an egg and it smashes, you may have good news. If, however, the egg merely cracks or is still in one piece, bad luck may befall you.

elder *see* TREES.

eyes the shape, the colour, the position and the amount of
white around the eye can all influence some people in
their 'reading' of a person's character. For example, a
person who has white showing under the pupils of his or
her eyes is said to be of noble character and laudable
lifestyle. Deep-set eyes are thought by some to indicate
shrewdness.

Brown eyes are supposed to be the kindest, whilst
blue-grey eyes indicate generosity. The list of attributes
is long and varies considerably. Perhaps it is fairest to
say that people are judged to some extent by their appearance and features that appeal to some will not be at-
tractive to others.

If your right eye itches, it is said that you are about to
suffer a disappointment. If the left eye itches, things
look more promising—you could be in for a pleasant
surprise!

Styes are a painful and fairly common affliction of the
eye. They will disappear of their own accord, but many
people believe it to be helpful to rub the stye gently with
a gold ring.

F
feet it is considered to be luckier to put your right foot out
of bed first in the morning.

If your feet are itchy, you may be about to go on a journey.

If you wear your shoes out on the inside of the foot
first, it is said that you are mean. If you wear them out

on the outside of the foot first, you may be inclined to be extravagant.

Flirts, it is said, will wear out the toes of their shoes first.

fingers it is, of course, wrong to tell a lie, but if you cross your fingers whilst you lie, some of the harm will be undone, it is said.

If two people say the same word at exactly the same time, they should link the little fingers of their right hands together, make a wish, and say the name of a poet. Their wishes will come true only if they each utter the name of a different poet.

fire fires should never be raked out completely at the end of the day. One or two embers should be left in the grate to stave off misfortune.

fish the best way to eat a fish is believed to be starting at the tail and working towards the head.

The haddock is considered to be a lucky fish. Scottish folklore holds that the haddock was the fish used in the feeding of the five thousand. The two black spots at either side of a haddock's head are said to be the marks left by the thumb and forefinger of Christ.

first foot *see* NEW YEAR; COAL.

flowers there are countless superstitions concerning flowers, their meanings and their properties. The following examples are a selection of some of these.

Many nurses take great pains to avoid combining red and white flowers in the same vase in their hospital wards—this combination is said to be very unlucky and signify death. It is also considered to be unlucky for hospital patients to take home their flowers when they are discharged. It is said to mean that they will soon be back in their hospital bed.

Picking up a flower that someone else has cut or picked and then dropped is said to be unlucky.

clover: the belief that finding a four-leafed clover brings good luck to the finder is widespread. If the finder then passes the clover onto someone else, it is said that his or her good luck will increase.

daffodil: it is unlucky to pick and take a single daffodil inside. Always take a bunch.

daisy: it is said that girls can find out the true feelings of their sweethearts by picking a daisy and plucking out the petals one by one, saying alternately with each petal plucked, 'He loves me, he loves me not.'

dandelion: use a dandelion seed-head if you want to find out if the one you love loves you. Blow away the seeds and with each puff say alternately, 'He loves me, he loves me not.'

If you want to find out how many years it will be until you marry the one you love, count the number of puffs it takes until all the seeds have gone.

gorse: the flowers of the gorse bush are unlucky to have in the house.

heather: white heather is considered by many people to be lucky, but it is better to grow it than to buy it.

lilac: white lilac flowers are considered to be unlucky and should not be taken into the house.

marigold: if you pick marigolds that you have grown yourself, it is said that you will become a drunkard.

may: bringing May blossom into the house will bring bad luck, it is said.

orange blossom: orange blossom is traditionally considered to be lucky to have at a wedding. It has associations with fertility.

pansies: picking pansies when it is sunny is said to cause rain.

poppies: never take poppies into the house because they are considered by some to be quite unlucky in this instance. It is also believed that staring into the centre of a poppy will cause temporary loss of vision, although it could be argued that staring hard at anything will bring this about.

snowdrops: although a harbinger of spring and hence of new life, snowdrops are thought to be unlucky to have in the house, particularly if there is a sick person within.
See also PLANTS, TREES and BUSHES.

fork if you inadvertently cross two forks over one another, you may take it as a sign that you may be the subject of malicious gossip and slander in time to come.

If you drop a fork, you can expect a visit from a woman friend.

Stirring with a fork instead of a spoon is considered to be unlucky.

food and drink making the tea weaker than usual may be an indication that a friend is turning away from you.

If the coffee pot rocks while it heats on the stove a visitor will be coming, it is said.

If the soup continues to boil after you have taken it off the cooker it is a sign that you will live to a ripe old age.

If the bread that you are baking burns, it is said to be a sign that someone is angry with you.

If a cork pops out of a bottle suddenly, beware, for you have a secret enemy.

The wine should always be passed round the table to the right, in a clockwise direction, following the course of the sun.

Do not fret if you drop a custard pie or any other pie in which eggs are ingredients. If it falls to the floor, you may be destined to be rich! *See also* EGGS, CHRISTMAS, FISH.

G

geese *see* BIRDS.

glass it is not unlucky to break glass unless it is in the form of a bottle or a mirror, or if it is coloured. Breaking a mirror is particularly unlucky as it carries seven years of bad luck. It is said that breaking red glass invites troubles and worries in the future, and breaking green glass means future disappointment. *See also* BOTTLE.

gloves it is considered to be unlucky to give gloves as a gift unless you receive something in return. *See also* CLOTHES

If you drop your glove or gloves you should let someone else pick them up to avoid bad luck.

gorse *see* FLOWERS.

grass *see* PLANTS.

grave it is considered to be unlucky to tread on someone's grave, or to pick flowers from a grave. The first grave in a churchyard was often very hard to fill as it was believed that the first corpse buried in a cemetery would be taken by the Devil. *See also* **death**.

green *see* COLOUR.

H

hair cuttings from a woman's hair should always be swept up and disposed of carefully. If they are left lying around, it is said that birds may come and take them for their nests and this would give the woman a headache.

It is considered to be luckier to have one's hair cut when the moon is waxing, preferably when it is new.

The term 'widow's peak' stems from the belief that a woman whose hair grew into a point on her forehead was destined to become a widow.

Hallowe'en if a girl wishes to see who her future lover will be, she should try sitting alone in front of a mirror in candlelight on Hallowe'en, eating an apple. A vision of her true love should appear in the mirror, looking over her shoulder towards the glass. The girl should not turn round, but should go on eating the apple and looking into the mirror until the vision fades.

To answer any questions on Hallowe'en, run a new silk thread through a gold ring and hold it over a tumbler of water. Ask one question that can be answered with a direct 'yes' or 'no'. Hold the ends of the thread steadily as you ask, then notice how many times the ring strikes against the glass. If once, the answer is 'no'. If the ring strikes the glass twice, the answer is 'maybe', and if the ring strikes the glass three times, the answer is 'yes'. *See also* BABIES.

hand if the palm of your hand is itchy, it is said that you are going to be rich. It is also said that rubbing the itchy hand on wood is a way of ensuring that the wealth actually comes to you.

handkerchief tying a knot in a handkerchief is widely recognized as a trick to prod the memory. But it is also thought to be a way of protecting oneself from evil spirits.

Picking up a handkerchief you have dropped yourself is thought by some to be unlucky.

hare *see* ANIMALS.

heather *see* FLOWERS.

hedgehog *see* ANIMALS.

hen *see* BIRDS.

horse *see* ANIMALS.

horse chestnut *see* TREES AND BUSHES.

horseshoe *see* HORSE.

I

ink it is generally believed to be quite unlucky, as well as annoying, to spill ink.

insects There are various superstitions connected with insects.

ants: it is quite commonly believed that to step on an ant will cause rain to come.

bees: many people, especially in rural areas, believe that it is unlucky to kill a bee.

A swarm of bees that appears from nowhere and lands on your property is thought to be unlucky, foretelling death, but it is lucky to be given a hive of bees as a gift.

beetles: as with ants, it is believed that stepping on beetles will bring wet weather.

ladybirds: ladybirds are generally considered to be lucky creatures, and you are very fortunate if one of these delightful little insects lands on you.

ivy *see* PLANTS.

J

jacket *see* CLOTHES.

January *see* MONTHS.

journey *see* feet; NAILS.

Judas *see* ELDER TREE; THIRTEEN.

K

knife some say that it is unlucky if two knives are crossed by chance, for it is seen as a bad sign, foretelling quarrelling, or worse.

If a knife falls to the floor and ends up with its blade sticking in the floor, it can be taken as a sign, it is said, that a visitor is on the way.

Spinning a knife on the table is also thought to be unlucky.

knots it was an old tradition of midwives to undo any knots and fastenings on the clothes of a woman who was giving birth. This practice was believed to ease the passage of the child into the world.

Some people believe that the knots in the clothing or in the shroud of a dead person should all be untied before the person is buried, to enable the dead person's soul to pass freely from one world to the next.

L

ladder the belief that it is unlucky to walk under a ladder is possibly one of the most widely known superstitions and is one that is believed by a great number of people, although most of them will not know why it is supposed to be so unlucky. The superstition possibly stems from the fact that when a ladder is raised up against a wall, it forms a triangle with the wall and the ground. The triangle is seen as representing the Holy Trinity and to walk through this is seen as an affront to God. As to what will happen to you if you do walk under a ladder, accounts vary. Some say that young girls who walk under ladders will never marry. Some take the act as an omen of death. Others see it as a portent of bad luck in general.

ladybirds *see* INSECTS.

lamb *see* ANIMALS.

laughter laughter before breakfast, it is said, will bring tears before nightfall.

lilac *see* FLOWERS

lips tingling lips are said to be sign that you will soon be kissed by somebody.

M

magpie *see* BIRDS.

March *see* MONTHS.

marigold *see* FLOWERS.

mandrake *see* PLANTS.

May *see* MONTHS.

may *see* FLOWERS.

mirror the breaking of a mirror will bring seven years of bad luck down upon the person who breaks it. *See also* GLASS.

It is believed that a child who sees its own reflection in a mirror before it is six months (some say a year) old will not live long. *See also* BABY.

It is considered unlucky for a bride to look at her reflection in a mirror when she is dressed in her wedding clothes, before she is married.

Some people consider it to be unlucky to look at their reflection in a mirror after dark, or by candlelight.

mistletoe *see* PLANTS; CHRISTMAS.

months

January: A mild January is supposed by some to be a forecast of a poor harvest.

Children who are born on New Year's day are considered to be lucky for the household into which they are born.

March: It is believed that a wet March will mean a poor harvest that year.

May: Some people believe that it is unlucky to get married in the month of May.

moon the moon was associated in days past with an influence on the growth of hair and nails. From this stems the superstition that it is best to have your hair cut while the moon is waxing so that it grows strong and healthy. The same applies to the cutting of nails. *See also* NAILS.

It is believed by some that it is wrong to point at the moon.

Some country folk still hold firm to the belief that it is best to sow seeds while the moon is on the increase.

It is considered by some to be unlucky for a child to be born when the moon is on the wane.

Some people used to believe that it was dangerous to sleep in the moonlight or to face the moon whilst sleeping, for it led to blindness or being 'moonstruck', a mild form of madness.

'Washing' your hands in moonlight was thought by some to be a cure for warts.

It is thought to be unlucky to see a new moon for the first time through a window.

A wish made while looking up at a new moon is said to come true before the end of the year.

mouse *see* ANIMALS.

mule *see* ANIMALS.

murder it was believed that a piece of ground on which a murder had been committed would never be fertile again.

mushrooms *see* PLANTS.

myrtle *see* PLANTS.

N

nails it is best to cut your nails while the moon is on the increase if you want them to grow strong. If you worry about which day to choose for cutting your nails, the following rhyme may help:

> *Cut your nails on Monday, cut them for news;*
> *Cut them on Tuesday for a new pair of shoes;*
> *Cut them on Wednesday, cut them for health;*
> *Cut them on Thursday, cut them for wealth;*

Cut them on Friday, a sweetheart to know;
Cut them on Saturday, a journey to go;
Cut them on Sunday, you cut them for evil,
For all the next week you'll be ruled by the Devil.

New Year just before midnight strikes on New Year's Eve, open a window in your house to let the Old Year out and the New Year in.

The first person to set foot in your house in the New Year should be a dark man. It is also believed that this man, the 'first foot', should not enter the house through the same door by which he came in; if he comes in the back door, he should leave by the front and vice versa.

It is thought to be unlucky to take something out of the house at New Year unless something has been brought in first. This should preferably be a lump of coal. Thus, the best thing to happen to a household at New Year is for a dark man to arrive after the stroke of midnight, carrying a lump of coal.

It is thought unlucky for your first visitor of the New Year to be fair-haired, or, worse still, a woman!

If your cupboards are not well stocked at New Year, you may go hungry in the coming twelve months.

It is thought to be advisable to wind up all the clocks in the house to ensure good luck, and to clean the house thoroughly on New Year's Eve. *See also* MONTHS

nose a nose bleed is thought by some to be a sign that the afflicted person is close to another for whom they feel a great deal of affection, perhaps someone with whom they are in love.

An itchy nose is said, according to different schools of thought, to be either a sign that you are angry, or that you will have a quarrel, or that you will be kissed by a fool, or that you will receive news or a letter.

nuns meeting a nun on the street is thought by some to be unlucky. Fishermen have even postponed a day at sea because they have passed a nun on their way to the boat.

More specifically, it is believed by some that it is unlucky to look at the *back* of a nun.

Some believe that spitting is a way to ward off the bad luck that seeing a nun can bring.

Three nuns, on the other hand, appear to be a luckier combination.

O

oak *see* TREES.

orange if someone gives an orange to their sweetheart, it should help the progress of their love affair. *See also* COLOUR.

orange blossom *see* FLOWERS.

owl *see* BIRDS.

P

palm the crosses made from palm that people receive in church on Palm Sunday came to be attributed with the power of keeping evil spirits and witchcraft at bay, and were carefully preserved until the next year.

pancakes pancakes are the traditional fare of Shrove Tuesday and if eaten on this day, they are thought to give you luck for the coming year. You are unlikely to have an empty stomach or an empty purse.

It is said, however, that you are best to eat the pancake after eight o'clock at night.

pansies *see* FLOWERS.

peacock *see* BIRDS.

petticoat if a girl's petticoat hangs down below her dress, it is believed that her father loves her better than her mother does.

picture if a picture falls from its hanging-place, it can be taken as a bad omen. If the picture is a portrait of a family member, it is an omen of death.

Some people consider it unlucky to hang a picture either over a door or over a bed.

pins

> See a pin and pick it up,
> All the day you'll have good luck.
> See a pin and let it lie,
> Luck will surely pass you by.

If you spill a box of pins, try to ensure that you prevent some of them from falling out. If some pins are left in the box, you may get a pleasant surprise. If all the pins fall out of the box, you are likely to suffer a disappointment.

plants *bracken*: bracken is thought to be lucky to hang in the house. It is said to protect the building against the effects of thunder and lightning.

Destroying bracken is thought to cause wet weather.

chicory: the chicory plant is considered by some to bring good luck to travellers if they carry a root of the plant in their pocket.

grass: when a dog or a cat eats grass, it may be taken as an omen of rain on the way.

ivy: ivy is thought to be a lucky plant to have growing on the walls of your house. Ivy inside the house, on the other hand, is thought by some people to be unlucky, even if it is for the Christmas decorations!

mandrake: the mandrake plant has a strange-shaped root that is said by some to resemble the shape of a human. Folklore tells that when a mandrake root is pulled up, it emits a terrible shrieking sound. For this reason, many people avoided trying to dig up this plant. However, it was also thought to have curative properties and was used in various sorts of medicaments. In order for the screaming of the roots to be avoided, it was believed to be best to have the plant dug up by a dog.

mistletoe: mistletoe is thought of as part of the traditional Christmas decorations, but it should not be hung in church because of its ancient associations with the Druids, to whom the plant was sacred.

Kissing under the mistletoe at Christmas time is said to guarantee lifelong friendship with those whom you kiss and it is considered to be unlucky to refuse to be kissed under the mistletoe. *See also* CHRISTMAS.

mushrooms: if you grow mushrooms, you should not check on the progress of your crop until you feel that it should be mature, for superstition holds that mushrooms that have been looked at will not grow any more!

myrtle: myrtle is considered to be a plant symbolic of love. Myrtle that grows in your garden should be carefully tended, for to allow it to die is to invite ill-fortune.

rosemary: a branch of rosemary hung at the door, or rosemary growing near the door, is said protect the house from evil spirits and plague.

Sprigs of rosemary in the bridal bouquet should bring happiness at a wedding.

sage: sage is said to be helpful in practices of divination. If a girl wishes to know who she will marry, she can go out at midnight on Hallowe'en and pluck nine sage leaves, as the clock strikes the hour. Then she should be able to see the face of her future husband.

plate it is a sign of bad luck to come to break a plate.

poppies *see* FLOWERS.

purse if you give someone a purse as a gift, you should always put a coin inside it before you give it to the person. To fail to do this is to condemn them to a life without riches, it is said.

R

rabbit *see* ANIMALS.

raven *see* BIRDS.

red *see* COLOUR.

reflection *see* MIRROR.

robin *see* BIRDS.

rocking an empty cradle *see* BABIES.

rosemary *see* PLANTS.

rowan *see* TREES AND BUSHES.

S

sage *see* PLANTS.

sailors sailors are notoriously superstitious, probably because of the dangers that a life at sea used to entail in days of old. The custom of breaking a bottle of champagne on the prow of a vessel and blessing it when it is first launched has its origins in the fears that sailors of the past used to feel for the demons of the deep. What is now essentially a celebration of the ship's launch was before seen as an offering made to the gods. It is said to be bad luck if the bottle does not break at the first attempt to smash it.

People who die on board ship are traditionally buried at sea, for it was believed that it was bad luck to carry a body on board ship. When the body is committed to the waves, the sailors look away.

Women are supposed to be unlucky to have on board a working ship at sea.

The sound of a cat mewing on board ship is thought by some to be a bad omen.

Superstition says that it is lucky to touch a sailor, especially if you touch him on his collar.

salt spilling salt is thought to be unlucky. If you do spill some inadvertently, take a pinch of it and throw it over your left shoulder. It is thought that this practice could stem from a belief that the thrown salt would blind the Devil, who sits on the left. On the other hand, the practice could originate from times when salt was a valuable commodity. The throwing of the salt over the left shoulder could then be seen as a bribe for the Devil, to dissuade him from doing you any harm.

There is a superstition that if you borrow salt, you should not pay it back for this would be unlucky. Some people hold that the borrowing or lending of salt in itself is unlucky.

Throwing salt onto the fire is a practice intended to ward off witches.

A dish of salt placed on or by the corpse of a dead person was thought to protect the dead person in some way.

Bathing a new baby in salt water, or placing a small bag or sachet of salt somewhere about the baby's clothing, was thought to have a protective effect.

scissors if scissors are dropped by mistake and land standing up with their points sticking into the floor, it is a good sign.

If someone drops scissors, it is said that they would be well advised to leave someone else to pick them up.

shoes it is considered to be unlucky for a shoelace to break. If a shoelace comes undone by accident, however, provided that it has not been pulled out but has come undone by itself, it is a sign that your sweetheart is thinking of you.

It is thought to be unlucky to be given a pair of new shoes on Christmas Day.

Shoes on the table are said by some to be a sign that there will be a quarrel in the house. Others hold that shoes on the table mean thunder and lightning to come. Some merely consider them to bring bad luck in general.

It is considered to be unlucky to put the left shoe on first when getting dressed.

The relatively modern custom of tying old shoes (and assorted other rubbish) to the bumper of the newlyweds' car as they take off for honeymoon, may have its origins in an older custom of throwing old shoes at the newly married couple. *See also* FEET.

silver silver coins are generally thought to bring luck. The practice of keeping a lucky coin, particularly a silver one, is quite widespread.

The practice of crossing a gypsy's palm with silver was thought to act as a charm against evil, or at the very least, against the wrath of the gypsy!

singing singing before breakfast or during a meal is thought to be unlucky. This is also true for laughter.

Folklore tells us that singing before breakfast means tears at bedtime, while singing during a meal will only invite disappointment.

sneezing

> *Sneeze on Monday, sneeze for danger;*
> *Sneeze on Tuesday, kiss a stranger;*
> *Sneeze on Wednesday, get a letter;*
> *Sneeze on Thursday, something better;*
> *Sneeze on Friday, sneeze for sorrow;*
> *Sneeze on Saturday, see your true love tomorrow;*
> *Sneeze on Sunday, the Devil will have you for the rest of the week.*

It is thought that one sneeze is unlucky, but two are lucky.

The custom of saying 'bless you' to someone who sneezes probably has its origins in the days of the plague, when sneezing was one of the first signs of the dreaded illness. As the plague almost inevitably ended in death, the blessing was more of an acknowledgement of the sneezing person's approaching demise. *See also* ANIMALS, CAT

snowdrop *see* FLOWER.

spider killing a spider is widely thought to bring on the rain. Finding a little red money-spider on you can be taken as an indication of coming good fortune.

spit spitting has long been used as a way to drive away demons and fend off ill-fortune. Fasting spittle, that is the spittle of a person newly-risen from bed who had not eaten since the previous day, was at one time believed to have great curative powers, being recommended for ailments as varied as rashes, cuts and bruises, birthmarks and short-sightedness.

T

theatre actors and actresses are very superstitious by and large.

You should never wish actors good luck before they go on stage. Instead, it is traditional to say, 'Break a leg.'

Some plays are considered to be lucky plays, while some are thought to be very unlucky indeed. Shakespeare's *Macbeth*, in particular, is thought to be an unlucky play and is often simply referred to as 'that play', or 'the Scottish play' rather than by name.

Yellow is considered to be an unlucky colour to wear on stage; green is also associated by some with misfortune. *See also* COLOURS.

Fresh flowers are unlucky according to theatrical tradition. Only artificial flowers should be used on stage.

Theatres with a dressing room number thirteen would be hard pushed to find someone willing to occupy it! *See also* WHISTLING.

thirteen thirteen is widely thought of as an unlucky number. Judas was the thirteenth man at the Last Supper, and it was he who betrayed Jesus and brought about his death. Because of this, it is believed to be most unlucky to have thirteen people dining at the table together. Some believe that the setting of a fourteenth place will stave off misfortune, but most people who are superstitious will simply refuse to hold a dinner party, or to attend a meal at which thirteen people are present.

Many hotels do not have a room number thirteen, and some streets do not have a house with that number.

Some people will go to quite extraordinary lengths to avoid having anything to do with the number thirteen.

three the number three is generally considered to be a lucky number; most people will probably have used or at least heard the expression 'third time lucky' at some time in their lives.

touch wood when we say 'touch wood', we should always do so as we touch something wooden with the right hand. This saying indicates some uncertainty on the behalf of the person saying it that they are totally responsible for their own destinies. Things may look to be going well, but just in case…

trees and bushes to catch an autumn leaf before it falls to the ground before the end of October is thought to be lucky.

aspen: the aspen is well known as the tree that still

trembles with shame as it remembers its wood being used for the cross on which Jesus was crucified. It was also believed to be a cure for ague, or 'flu. The sufferer was supposed to cut a strand of hair and tie it to an aspen tree, saying, 'Aspen tree, Aspen tree, shake and shiver instead of me'.

blackberry: the blackberry bush can be bowed over into an arch under which people may pass if they wish to find a cure for rheumatism, warts and other ailments.

elder: sprigs from the elder tree should not be taken into the house for they are unlucky, it is said. It is believed that Judas hanged himself from an elder tree.

horse chestnut: the horse chestnut tree is believed to have certain curative properties and people sometimes carry conkers in their pockets to ease their rheumatism.

oak: It was once thought possible to transfer one's toothache to an oak tree by cutting a lock of hair and placing it in a hole in the tree, simultaneously entreating the tree to take the toothache.

It is thought to be unlucky to chop down an oak tree.

rowan: this tree has long been considered to be effective in warding off evil spirits. For this reason it is often to be found at the gates of graveyards, or growing by the door or gate of a house, particularly in rural areas.

U

umbrella it is thought to be unlucky to open an umbrella indoors.

Some say that to open an umbrella when the weather is fair is to invite rain.

If you drop an umbrella or a walking-stick, you should let someone else pick it up for you.

urine in days gone drops of urine would be sprinkled about the house or over the bed of a woman in labour as a protection against evil spirits. When somebody was suffering from a mysterious ailment and was thought to be bewitched, a sample of his or her urine was sealed in a bottle along with some pins, needles and nails and was then buried. This was supposed to make the witch's strength fail and thereby allow the person to be cured.

It has been said that if two lovers urinate at the same time it is unlucky and they will quarrel.

W

weddings weddings that take place in May are thought to be ill-fated. *See also* MONTHS.

It is said that whichever one of the bride and groom is the first to fall asleep on the night after the wedding, she or he will die first.

Wedding cake is customarily shared out among the guests on the wedding day to give them good luck. Girls who received a slice of wedding cake and put it under their pillows might be lucky enough to see their own future husband appear to them as they slept.

A flight of birds seen flying overhead by the bride on the morning of her wedding is said to be a sign of a happy marriage, with children to come.

It is unlucky for the bridegroom to see his future bride in her wedding dress before the marriage ceremony. For him to see the bride before the wedding on the wedding day, whatever she is wearing, is also thought by a great many people to be unlucky.

When dressing for her big day, it is customary for the bride to take heed of the following rhyme:

Something old, something new,
Something borrowed and something blue—
See that the church is full to the brim
Before the bride is allowed to come in.

When setting the date of their wedding, the couple might care to acknowledge the following rhyme:

Monday for health,
Tuesday for wealth;
Wednesday the best day of all;
Thursday for losses,
Friday for crosses;
Saturday, no luck at all!

Once married, you should keep your wedding ring safely on your finger, for it is considered to be unlucky to remove it.

whistling the sound of whistling may be a cheerful one, but it is traditionally feared in certain places. Whistling down a mine, for example, is considered to be very unlucky, likely to cause a catastrophe such as the roof caving in.

Whistling in a theatre should also be avoided, according to superstition. *See also* THEATRE.

It was believed that if a sailor whistled on board ship while out at sea, he would summon a gale.